BETWEEN THE LIES

RISE OF THE MEDIA-MILITARY-INDUSTRIAL COMPLEX

BETWEEN THE LIES

RISE OF THE MEDIA-MILITARY-INDUSTRIAL COMPLEX

Stan Winer

SOUTHERN UNIVERSITIES PRESS

Published in 2004
by *Southern Universities Press*

12 Mcleod Court
Dulwich Common
London SE22 8NS
UK

First published in March 2004 by SUPERSCRIPT,
then electronically in June 2004 at www.coldtype.net,
under the title *If Truth be Told*

This retitled and extended SUP edition, October 2004

ISBN 0 9545805 32

Cover design: idz.info

Printed in UK by
Antony Rowe Ltd, Eastbourne

Distributed by Gardners Books: www.gardners.com

The daily press and the telegraph, which in a moment spread inventions over the whole earth, fabricate more myths ... in one day than could have formerly been done in a century.

—— Karl Marx, 1871

... the attempt is always made to ensure that force will appear to be based on the consent of the majority, expressed by the so-called organs of public opinion — newspapers ...

—— Antonio Gramsci,
Prison Notebooks, 1929-1937

It is the absolute right of the State to supervise the formation of public opinion.

If you tell a lie big enough and keep repeating it, people will eventually come to believe it.

The lie can be maintained only for such time as the State can shield the people from the political, economic and/or military consequences of the lie. It thus becomes vitally important for the State to use all of its powers to repress dissent, for the truth is the mortal enemy of the lie, and thus by extension, the truth is the greatest enemy of the State.

—— Joseph Goebbels,
German Propaganda Minister, 1933-1945

For the forgotten heroes

Acknowledgements

Staff members at various libraries and archives provided invaluable help during the research for this book, particularly at the British Library Reading Room in London, the British Newspaper Library in Colindale, the British Public Records Office in Kew, the Open University library in Milton Keynes, and the University of London library in Bloomsbury.

Contents

Introduction

In a rare moment of candour in late August 2004, United States President George W Bush confessed to the American public and the world at large that he and his administration had "miscalculated" the disastrous consequences of invading Iraq. Bush could not say for sure "what went wrong", preferring instead to leave that "for the historians to decide." He somehow managed to overlook the fact that his administration had already placed a 25 years embargo on much of the official documentation upon which "the historians" would need to rely.

The politics of history and the integration of history into political transformation are therefore unlikely to receive any immediate boost from Bush's new-found openness. It is hoped, in the mean time, that *Between the Lies* might go some way towards filling in some of the existing, historical gaps.

Nor is Bush's belated show of honesty likely to change an already prevalent view among large numbers of people that they were duped by what the British and American governments had told them about the "war against terrorism" and about "weapons of mass destruction hidden in Iraq". In fact, many people today no longer believe much of what those governments say about anything else. Yet, while this public mood of disenchantment with politics and politicians may be a comparatively recent phenomenon, the military-political lies and deceptions that caused it are not something new, or something that arrived fully fledged and out of the blue. The official fabrications that "justified" the United States-led invasion of Iraq were but the most recent manifestation in a long continuum, namely the battle for public opinion in time of war. Today's official lies, as the following pages will show, seem almost benign when compared with, among other things, some of the secret propaganda operations hatched during World War II by Winston Churchill, and propagated by subservient mass media.

The pages that follow also provide a critical reassessment of prevailing heroic notions and enduring myths about what the military and political leadership of the West ostensibly intended and did actually achieve during some of the major military operations of the 20th Century, culminating in today's much vaunted "war on terrorism". If there is a lesson to be learned from all this, it is that the generally accepted outcomes of World War II and the Cold War, in particular, are wrongly perceived as a triumph of the "forces of good" over the "forces of darkness". The modern world is at least better understood as having emerged as the result of hidden factors that were neither wanted nor anticipated by those who made the ultimate sacrifices.

Between the Lies relates history to current affairs in an explicit manner by tracing how we arrived from a society ordered around a worthwhile set of common values to today's social climate of political disengagement and cynicism over just about everything. "Democracy" has finally succeeded in subverting its own legitimacy.

If this book helps dispel at least some wartime myths and illusions that survive to this day, then it will have served a useful purpose. Only an accurately informed citizenry can provide the essential check on unbridled power that true democracy requires. To that end, the history that unfolds in the following pages should show what the modern world is really about — if not exhaustively so, then at least on the right track and verifiable in all major particulars. As the historian John Lewis Gaddis puts it: "We act in the present with a view to shaping the future only on the basis of what we know from the past. So we might as well try to know our recent history as best we can, however imperfect the exercise may be. An incomplete map is better than no map at all."[1]

The evidence presented in this work takes a great variety and depth of official and declassified military documents, memoirs and other material in the public domain, and draws it all together to expose some central features of the battle for public opinion in time of war. The structure of the chapters comprises a chronological succession of inter-related epochs showing where humanity has been, where it is heading, and the role of media in allowing history to unfold in the certain way it has. This concerns a problem not only of history but of all human experience: the problem of truth and illusion.

Prologue:

1898 - 1939

If we are to understand the past with a view to explaining the world around, then the violent explosion on the battleship *USS Maine* in the Bay of Havana on 15 February 1898, is a good place to start. The extraordinary circumstances surrounding that affair were a harbinger of conspiracy and cover-up in the corridors of power — the filth of an age turned unheroic — which would find resonance in many of the most important military operations of the twentieth century and beyond.

Well before disaster struck the *Maine*, an anti-Spanish campaign had been supported by US businessmen who had major investments in Cuba and were keen on ousting the Spaniards. But the public was not interested, and neither were journalists. When the *Maine* sank, however, press baron William Randolph Hearst, proprietor of the *New York Journal*, immediately accused the Spaniards of having mined its hull and denounced Spanish barbarism and "death camps". The popular press, without a shred of evidence to back their claims, followed suit. "Remember the Maine. To Hell with Spain", they exclaimed, calling for vengeance and devoting full pages of their newspapers every day for months to the subject. Sales of the *Journal* soared from 30,000 to 400,000, and then regularly topped a million. United States president William McKinley, bowing to public pressure, declared war on Spain. The sinking of the *Maine* became the US's justification for its annexation of Cuba, Puerto Rico, the Philippines and the island of Guam. Thirteen years later

1

a commission of inquiry found that the explosion on the *Maine* had in fact been caused by an accident aboard the ship – something that was deliberately kept quiet in the intervening years.[1]

The incident provides an early example of the power of the Press to set the political agenda, and it exemplifies the dynamics that existed between secrecy, public opinion, governance and subversive propaganda, even before the advent of modern technology.

Another useful example is the sinking of Cunard Line's luxury flagship *RMS Lusitania* in May 1915. The British government suppressed a fact-finding inquest after the *Lusitania* disaster and, to this day, many questions surrounding the affair remain unanswered. There is evidence of information tampering, and relevant documents concerning the *Lusitania* are missing from both the Admiralty and Cunard files, while American records have their own share of missing documents. Whatever the content of the missing files, it is certainly true that the death toll in the sinking of the *Lusitania* is rivalled in maritime history only by the *Titanic* disaster of three years earlier. Nor is there any doubt that the destruction of the *Lusitania* was one of the First World War's single largest civilian disasters. It had far-reaching effects, and the political repercussions were enormous. The propaganda opportunities it offered paved the way for bringing America directly into World War 1 on the side of Britain and France at a time when they were very close to defeat.

Nonetheless, the *Lusitania* affair is either glossed over or remains entirely absent from orthodox history books. Similarly, the real diplomatic history of the United States and Great Britain during this great crisis is not to be found in the archives of the US State Department. Revisionist historians, however, sifting though the scraps of information that somehow managed to escape the censors and the incinerators, have in recent times reconstructed a convincing account of circumstances surrounding the affair. The available evidence suggests strongly that the British Admiralty not only knew in advance that the attack on the *Lusitania* was likely, but did nothing to prevent it. The chronology of events speaks clearly for itself:[2]

On 1 May 1915, the *Lusitania*'s New York departure date, the German embassy in Washington warns American civilians not to book passage on the Lusitania. The embassy emphasises that the luxury liner is a British military reserve vessel and hence a legitimate target heading into hostile waters, and Americans should not be on board. The warning is disregarded. On May 5, two days before *Lusitania* enters the Irish Channel, German submarine U-20 rounds the south-west tip of Ireland. The submarine spots the British schooner *Earl of Lathom*, surfaces to warn its crew to abandon ship, and then destroys it with gunfire. The next day, as U-20 continues east in the Irish Channel, it fires two torpedoes at the *SS Candidate*, a 5,858-ton steamer from Liverpool. About two hours later, U-20 destroys another ship, the *SS Centurion*. The British Admiralty refrains from warning the *Lusitania* of these attacks taking place close to where the *Lusitania* is about to travel.

On May 7, the *Lusitania* unwittingly enters the Irish Channel. The British destroyer *HMS Juno* has been assigned to escort her through these dangerous waters but at the last minute, astonishingly, the *Juno* is recalled by the British Admiralty. It fails to make its rendezvous with the *Lusitania*, nor are any alternative measures instituted to protect the giant passenger liner. Running at reduced speed because of fog and without an escort, it comes into the periscope view of U-20 which fires one torpedo, hitting the *Lusitania* directly amidships. As the Germans are preparing to fire a second torpedo, there is a tremendous explosion inside the *Lusitania* which blows a large hole at the bottom of the great ship. It immediately takes on a heavy list to starboard and starts sinking bow first. The destroyer *HMS Juno* is berthed at the nearby Irish port of Queenstown when she receives a radio distress signal from the stricken luxury liner. *Juno* hurries out toward the *Lusitania*, but suddenly turns back while close enough to be seen by the survivors in the water. *Juno* has received an official recall signal radioed from the Admiralty. This contributes significantly to the final death toll. Eighteen minutes after being hit by the German torpedo, the *Lusitania* is completely submerged, with the loss of 1,198 lives, many of them American.

If the sinking of the *Lusitania* was indeed deliberately provoked or actively encouraged, then the chain of events would probably have been set in motion four months earlier. That was when Winston Churchill, as First Lord of the Admiralty, had ordered British merchant ships to fly American flags so the Germans would not know if they were really British or American. Churchill considered this a guarantee of safe passage because, with America still neutral, Germany would be reluctant to draw America into the war on the side of the Allies. The Germans were fully aware of this ploy. On a voyage leaving Liverpool on 16 January 1915 the *Lusitania* had already been involved in an international incident which gave the ship's presence in the North Atlantic a very high profile. The ship was travelling through rough seas, making passage for the Irish port of Queenstown when, fearing the possibility of a torpedo attack its captain hoisted the stars and stripes. The use of the US flag, however, came to the notice of the press and the incident made world news.

There was provocation from the American side as well. The United States government consistently violated its own neutrality laws by allowing war materials to be sent to Britain and France. According to its manifest on the day it was sunk, the *Lusitania* was carrying a large cargo of rifle ammunition, probably destined for the war front.

Against this background, it is reasonable to deduce that military and political strategists in Britain thought the sinking of a major passenger liner with Americans onboard would change the pacifist nature of the American public. They seemed prepared to do whatever was needed to bring the United States into war on the side of Great Britain, and the deliberately provoked sinking of an American ship by Germany would have been a most effective way of doing so. If this is so, it involved not direct and overt acts but rather acts of omission, neglect and ambivalence. A sense of complacency was fostered and the *Lusitania* was encouraged to enter a war zone where German submarines were known to be active.

Historian Diana Preston, in her definitive study of the *Lusitania* tragedy, concludes: "The truth was that no government, British, German or American, was entirely free of blame for the situation leading up to the attack. Nor in its wake, was any government hesitant to twist the facts, or use the disaster, to its own political ends."[3] Clearly, however, something highly irregular and never fully explained occurred in British naval circles at the highest level of command around the time the luxury liner was torpedoed. The attack on the *Lusitania*, if not deliberately provoked or actively encouraged by the British Admiralty, was at least allowed to proceed when it could have been prevented.

German propagandists, in the reverberations of public uproar and media activity that followed, tried to justify the sinking of the *Lusitania* by insisting that Britain was using an illegal blockade to stop American ships carrying food to Germany, and this was being done in order to starve Germany's civilian population. The suffering this caused, according to German statements, was much worse than the suffering of the victims of the *Lusitania* disaster. The Germans also claimed that Britain was using the *Lusitania* as an auxiliary transport for Canadian troops and munitions.

Prior to the sinking of the *Lusitania*, there had been great reluctance on the part of the American people to become involved in the war. In fact there was forthright admiration for the German leader Kaiser Wilhelm as evidenced by a special supplement devoted to the Kaiser in the New York Times on June 8, 1913, on the 25th anniversary of his coronation and shortly before the outbreak of World War 1. On its front page, along with a handsome portrait of the monarch in a Navy uniform, was an effusive salute to him from the paper's editors. The banner headline at the top read: KAISER, 25 YEARS A RULER, HAILED AS CHIEF PEACEMAKER. The accompanying story called him "the greatest factor for peace that our time can show" — and credited Wilhelm with frequently rescuing Europe from the brink of war.

Along with the Times's unstinting praise came effusive tributes from prominent Americans. These included Theodore Roosevelt, his White House successor William Howard Taft, Columbia University president Nicholas Murray Butler and steel tycoon Andrew Carnegie, whose full page commentary concluded that all the citizens of the civilised world were the Kaiser's "admiring loving debtors" for his "service to the cause of peace." However, when the *Lusitania* left New York Harbor on 1 May 1915, bound for Liverpool with 196 Americans on board and was sunk six days later off the coast of Ireland, many Americans were outraged that Germany could "without provocation" so ruthlessly attack a "civilian passenger ship". This act of barbarism, according to Colonel Edward M House, US president Woodrow Wilson's personal adviser at the time, left the United States no option other than to be at war with Germany "within a month".[4]

House's optimism was misplaced. The sinking of the *Lusitania* did not ignite sufficient public outrage in America to justify the country's immediate entry into the war. President Wilson had expressly been elected on a platform of keeping the US out of the European war. He did not even sever diplomatic ties with Germany over the sinking of the *Lusitania*, which drew derision from the British media. This was much to the embarrassment of Walter Page, the American ambassador in

London. He addressed to Wilson an increasingly irate stream of protests verging on insolence and complaining bitterly about the latter's "inaction".[5] Two years would elapse before America finally abandoned its neutrality and joined the Allies on April 16, 1917.

Pressure on the US administration was almost certainly also brought to bear from at least one section of Wall Street. As Georgetown University professor Carroll Quigley disclosed in his remarkable book *Tragedy and Hope*,[6] there existed by the time of the *Lusitania* affair an organisation of wealthy bankers and influential politicians headed by Lord Alfred Milner, who was Governor General and High Commissioner of South Africa and also a very powerful person in British banking and politics. This shadowy organisation, modelled along the lines of an elite secret society and virtually indistinguishable from a private empire within the British Empire covering half the globe, was fronted in Britain by the Royal Institute of International Affairs. In New York it was called the Council of Foreign Relations, fronted by the JP Morgan bank of which JP Morgan Jnr just happened to be Britain's purchasing agent for American-made munitions. As subscription agent for war loans to England and France, the bank had already floated about $1.5 billion in war bonds on behalf of England and a lesser amount for France. The only time war loans are repaid is when the nation borrowing the money wins the war. What would become of that $1.5 billion if Britain and France lost the war? It seems likely there was considerable pressure from Wall Street for the United States to enter the war.

Whatever the hidden pressures of vested interests that might have been brought to bear on the US administration after the *Lusitania* was attacked, the British Ministry of Information for its part began energetically aiming overt propaganda at American opinion and opinion leaders. The Wilson administration followed suit by setting up the Committee on Public Information, America's first state propaganda agency. Members of Wilson's propaganda agency included people like Edward Bernays, who later became a leading figure in the American public relations industry, and Walter Lippmann, one of America's most respected journalists, who supported the "manufacture of consent" by a "specialised class" of people using propaganda.[7] Bernays, for his part, held that it was the "essence of democracy" for "the more intelligent members" of society to drive the general population into believing whatever "the more intelligent members" wanted the population to believe.[8] In other words, ordinary tax-paying people were not considered to be the best judges of their own interests and were in effect excluded from any real influence in the democratic, political decision-making process. Yet, both then as now, supposedly democratic nations would continue to undermine and subvert their own legitimacy, which is purportedly conferred by democratic consensual opinion.

Meanwhile, the propaganda war against Germany had in fact started on the eve of World War 1 — two years before the Lusitania tragedy — when the British public was fed a diet of official lies, exaggerations and half-truths to justify Britain's entry into the war. A British Parliamentary War Aims Committee convinced the public that Britain was being reluctantly pulled into war by the barbarism of the Germans who had just invaded Belgium. This committee, as Phillip Knightley has described it in his extraordinary book *The First Casualty*, was responsible for spreading wild rumours about the invasion. Belgian nuns were reportedly violated, children mutilated and thousands of innocent civilians lined up and slaughtered.[9] In 1915, a further committee of supposedly independent lawyers and historians under Lord Bryce, Britain's former ambassador to the USA, produced the Bryce Report into alleged German atrocities. It did everything it could to create public animosity against the Germans with a timeless ploy — the atrocity story. Murder, lust and pillage, according to the report were occurring "on a scale unparalleled in any war between civilised nations during the last three centuries."

The report contained stories of how German officers had publicly gang-raped 20 Belgian girls in a marketplace, how eight German soldiers had bayoneted a two-year-old child, and how one soldier had sliced off a Belgian peasant girl's breasts.[10] The newspapers, particularly *The Times* and the *Daily Mail* under the proprietorship of Lord Northcliffe had a field day, carrying illustrations of Germans beheading babies and eating their flesh.

The Bryce Report was translated into 30 languages, and used to show the world that Britain was acting honourably in defending Belgium against the barbarism of the Germans — rather than expanding its own interests, which included grabbing German colonial territories in Africa and adding them to the British Empire. A war aimed at imperial expansion was thus disguised as a necessary action against an unprincipled aggressor. A Belgian commission of enquiry in 1922 would be unable to corroborate even one major allegation in the Bryce Report.

This kind of thing was not new to British propagandists. By the time of the Bryce Report, they had already gained much experience in the first major conflict of the twentieth century — the South African war of 1899 to 1902. That was when the British government succeeded in disguising an unpopular war aimed at expanding British imperial interests as a decent British attempt to put down the "barbarous" Boers. British officials and the decent British public at large somehow managed to overlook the fact that more than 26,000 Boer women and children were at that time dying of diseases, exposure and malnutrition in Lord Kitchener's concentration camps, the first such camps of modern times.

Hitler, for one, was very impressed with British propaganda. In *Mein Kampf* he would argue that propaganda was the real victor in World War I and vowed that next time around Germany would be ready with its own propaganda systems modelled on those of the democracies.

Both then as now, there was however no general public

awareness of the dynamics that exist between governance, secrecy, public opinion and the media. It was and probably still is not generally known how propaganda works, how it is used to shape attitudes and opinions and induce conformity and subordination to the official line. This sort of information is not actively encouraged to enter the Anglo-Saxon consciousness. Nor does politically convenient historiography encourage the taking into account of shades of grey. Only black-and-white is permitted. The consequences are historical illiteracy and portrayals by the media of war crimes and crimes against humanity that are all too often reduced to a simplistic, lop-sided cowboy morality of white hats triumphing over black hats.

The roots of this kind of Anglo-Saxon moral triumphalism can probably be traced back to early New England, where the massacre of American Indians as "heathens" and "primitive savages" set the pattern for the self-justified slaughter of external enemies — a ritual that would be endlessly replayed as cultural infantilism not only in fiction, movies, toys and comics, but also and especially in real life. Ordinary folk were thus encouraged to structure their national identity via slaughter and the triumph of "good over evil". This fits neatly into their black-and-white universe.

Perhaps people need their myths about the "bad guys" in order to objectify their primal fears outside of themselves where they can "deal" with them. But let us not fool ourselves that a black-hats-white-hats mentality is good for you, or that such a value system has any real weight. Ancient historians such as Tacitus had no difficulty in grasping this. They knew perfectly well that history may be an argument without end, but it should nonetheless advance towards at least an approximation of the truth by sifting and assessing conflicting evidence.

Some modern historians are culturally infantile by comparison with historians of the Heroic Age. Works of modern history are frequently so tainted and ideologically loaded as to be worthless. If the past is a foreign country, then some latter-day historians have not even ventured beyond their front door. They overstate official versions of the past by advancing them for political reasons and purposes, repeating claims they cannot substantiate, and mining resources to find evidence bolstering their arguments while ignoring counter-evidence. Such methods encourage the abuse of history in constructing "national identities", and they propagate a view that history must be told on the basis of official documents or not be told at all.

This much is clear from facile versions of wartime events of the 20th Century and beyond, which perpetuate the worst aspects of nationalistic and ideological conflict: dehumanising the Other through stereotype.

That peculiar way of thinking – which is also the body politic of the military-industrial complex — provides an ideal breeding ground for the unscrupulous exploitation of collective states of mind, while favouring the covert achievement of political objectives through the subversion of democracy. It is directed towards enemy, friendly and neutral audiences alike; and it is a vast, grey, almost boundless area in which standards of decency do not apply. Above all, it typifies a two-tier system of governance: the subversion of truth on one tier while the other preserves its outward form. The first tier is usually the decisive one.

It was, for instance, a comparatively small covert operation carried out one dark night in 1939 that precipitated the most calamitous episode in the history of the world. Nazi SS troopers disguised in Polish army uniforms faked an attack on the radio broadcasting station at Gleiwitz in Upper Silesia on the German side of the border with Poland. They seized the radio station, announced in Polish that "Poles" were attacking, transmitted a short inflammatory speech in Polish, fired some shots, dumped a few bodies of Polish prisoners dressed in Polish uniforms, and then left before the night was out. The world awakened a few hours later to the astonishing news that the Polish Army had launched an unprovoked attack on the Third Reich. It served as Hitler's justification for the mobilisation of German aggression and the invasion of Poland that followed, sparking off World War II.[11]

By the time the slaughter of World War II ended, an estimated 50 million people would have been shot, bombed, drowned, frozen or starved to death.[12] Clearly, disinformation or subversive propaganda can achieve large results with disproportionately small effort.

Part One

WORLD WAR II: 1940 — 1943

Chapter 1:

Manufacturing Hate

Nearly all the major military operations of World War II were shrouded in such extreme secrecy that most servicemen on the Allied side had very little idea of how the many individual actions and campaigns in which they were engaged fitted into the overall strategic pattern. Winston Churchill made a classic understatement when, six years before the outbreak of World War II, he admitted: "There are many kinds of manoeuvres in war, some only of which take place upon the battlefield."[1] Few of those who did the actual fighting and dying had much idea of what they were actually involved in beyond fighting Hitler and Nazis. Others knew exactly what they were doing, but kept quiet because their revelations would seem so incredibly outrageous that nobody would believe them anyway. The Official Secrets Act also ensured that lips would remain tightly sealed even long after the war ended. Above all, "patriotism" and a perceived need to protect "the national interest" combined with censorship to retain a wall of silence around many major wartime operations.

Those who were motivated by a belief in the war as an honourable crusade for humanity against Evil, thought they were fighting and dying for a cause worth fighting and dying for. But as the following pages will show, their military and political leadership lied often and unashamedly both to the Allied armed forces and to the Western society of nations at large. The result has been historical illiteracy and engulfing public ignorance about the past, not least in relation to what really happened on the moonlit night of November 14, 1940, when repeated waves of Heinkel bombers took off from airfields in Germany and in German-occupied Europe. Their target in this, the *Luftwaffe*'s heaviest air raid of the war so far, was Coventry in the industrial heart of the English Midlands.

The Heinkels numbering 449 in all were not embarked on what may truthfully be described as a surprise attack. British codebreakers, in an extremely secret operation codenamed Ultra, had for the past seven months already been secretly intercepting and deciphering German military radio communications at every level of command, from the highest level down to regimental command. It provided British Prime Minister and Defence Minister Winston Churchill and Britain's secret intelligence service MI-6 with a very decisive advantage: consistent and reliable advance knowledge of the enemy's military strength, disposition and likely behaviour. According to Squadron Leader Frederick W Winterbotham, the chief of Air Intelligence at MI-6 and Churchill's personal intelligence liaison officer, Ultra provided "the unique experience of knowing not only the precise composition, strength and location of the enemy's forces, but also, with few exceptions, of knowing beforehand exactly what he intended to do ...."[2]

So secret was this information, derived from the German "Enigma" cipher, that even Churchill's closest Cabinet colleagues including his Secretary for War, Anthony Eden, were at the time completely unaware of the existence of Ultra.[3] The British public would similarly be kept in the dark about Ultra for the next 30 years.[*] Neither Churchill's Cabinet colleagues nor the public thus had any idea that Churchill, through Ultra, had secretly been alerted to the impending attack even before the

---

[*] The British government attempted unsuccessfully in the early 1970s to suppress publication of Winterbotham's wartime memoirs, *The Ultra Secret, London;* (Weidenfeld and Nicolson), 1974.

heavily laden Heinkels took off — at least 48 hours before the first of the raiders arrived over Coventry.[4]

Churchill, armed with ample forewarning of the attack, did nothing to prevent it, or at the very least to minimise civilian casualties. He refrained deliberately from ordering an evacuation of the doomed city, nor did he order the RAF to launch a concerted attack on the Coventry-bound bombers when the raiders were at their most vulnerable: when the lumbering bombers were taking off from Germany. Even as the bombers were airborne, Churchill failed to mobilise effective Royal Air Force fighter formations even though the information provided by Ultra would have enabled the RAF to deploy fighter squadrons at exactly the right place, the right time, and at the right altitudes.

Although advanced electronic counter measures were available at the time, no attempt was made to jam the radio navigation beams used by the enemy bombers.[5] Similarly, British radar and anti-aircraft defences were not placed on optimum alert, civil defence and fire-fighting units were neither warned nor reinforced, and no extra mobile anti-aircraft batteries were moved into the area.*

Even when the Heinkels converged on Coventry, RAF night-fighter pilots were ordered expressly to attack the bombers only "on their homeward journey as they switch on their navigation lights", that is *after* the Germans have dropped their bombs.[6] In a sustained 10-hour attack, wave after wave of German bombers were thus permitted — encouraged even — to kill 554 people, seriously injure 865 others, and all but raze an undefended Coventry to the ground. No German bomber was

---

* Professor RV Jones, principal British intelligence scientific adviser on electronic counter measures during the war, confirmed in a 1988 interview with the author that a powerful radio transmitter used for jamming enemy navigation beams was inexplicably switched off by a person or persons unknown, for the duration of the Coventry raid.

shot down and only one was slightly damaged.[7] A predictable crescendo of public outrage followed, escalating greatly an already widespread public hatred for Germany. The national mood was appropriate for Churchill to order the RAF to select a city in Germany for immediate retaliation.[8] Few, however, suspected that some circumstances surrounding the attack on Coventry may have been deliberately contrived in order to inflame and incite public opinion, that the city was covertly sacrificed in order to justify RAF retaliation, and to "legitimise" future terror bombing operations against civilian targets in Germany.

Here commenced Britain's so-called "strategic air offensive". It would ultimately result in the deaths of 700,000 German civilians and thousands of the RAF Bomber Command's own courageous pilots and aircrew, without any overt military advantage to Britain. Only the *British Journal of Medical Psychology*, perhaps without even realising it, came close to the truth a couple of years later when it analysed how the psychology of hate-propaganda works:

> First fear is stirred up, then hate to keep it in check; but the hate expects retaliation and thus increases fear, which has to be drowned by more hate and so on. The system needs effective hate — hate which cannot be satisfied.

Diligent application by Churchill of a similar if not identical technique soon induced the collective British mood reflected in a classified Home Intelligence report in the wake of Coventry. It described the British public as unanimously wanting the RAF to "blow a bloody big hole where Berlin is".[10]

Thirty years later, when the existence of Ultra was eventually made public, apologists for Churchill would foster an enduring myth about the reason why Coventry had been sacrificed. They would argue that a spirited defence of the city would have alerted the Germans to the fact that the Enigma code had been broken; the Germans would then have been obliged to change the cipher, and this would have had a disastrous effect on Britain's intelligence operations. That line of reasoning is unconvincing. Churchill and the RAF had no similar reservations about using Ultra to their fullest advantage during the earlier, massed aerial attacks by *Luftwaffe* fighters seeking air supremacy of British skies in July and August 1940 — the so-named Battle of Britain, in which the RAF emerged victorious. Fully two weeks before the Battle of Britain, Churchill had broadcast a warning on BBC radio, openly alerting the public to the impending attacks.

That was three months before Coventry was sacrificed "to protect Ultra". Even earlier, in March 1941, Ultra had made possible Britain's first major naval victory of the war, when the Italian navy was wiped out at the Battle of Cape Matapan. As Churchill later described it, "This timely and welcome victory off Cape Matapan disposed of all challenge to British naval mastery in the Eastern Mediterranean at this critical time."[11] The branch of the secret intelligence service known as London Controlling Section, which operated within the Joint Planning Staff at Churchill's headquarters, was skilled in devising and co-ordinating strategic cover and deception operations in all theatres of war.[12] In the Battle of Matapan, LCS had utilised an RAF reconnaissance aircraft to deceive the Axis into believing that aerial reconnaissance rather than Ultra intercepts was responsible for pinpointing the whereabouts of the Italian fleet in the Mediterranean. It seems odd, to say the least, that Churchill had not instructed LCS to devise and execute a similar deception in the instance of Coventry. Or, if any deception operation did in fact take place, then the enemy was certainly not the intended target of such psychological warfare.

Another enduring myth fostered by Churchill and his apologists, including official historians, is that a proper defence of Coventry was impossible because Germany held a superior advantage in the numbers of military aircraft available. This was simply untrue. Reliable figures would disclose after the war that the RAF in 1940 held a significant 15.5% numerical advantage over the *Luftwaffe* in terms of fighter aircraft alone.[13]

Given their frequent resort to subterfuge and deceit, and their hollow excuses not only for the martyrdom of Coventry but for numerous subsequent military failures, it is reasonable to deduce that Churchill and at least some of his hand-picked advisers were embarked on a course of mass deception. At times their pervasive influence on the ebb and flow of war would be for short-term tactical gain, at other times it would be in pursuit of long-term strategic objectives which would only later become evident in that war called peace, the Cold War.

In the mean time, and although none of them approached the scale of the Coventry raid, Germany's air attacks on British ports and transportation centres continued unabated until June 1941, leaving in their wake about 30,000 British civilian dead. With Hitler's invasion of Russia, however, the Blitz on Britain ended abruptly with the *Luftwaffe* turning its attention to Russia, which now became. Britain's only fighting ally in Europe.

On the other side of the world, meanwhile, a mass deception was being set in motion that would bear a close resemblance to earlier circumstances surrounding the German attack on Coventry. As with the German raid on Coventry, the Japanese attack on Pearl Harbor on 7 December 1941 would have come as a surprise to its victims, but it could not have come as any great surprise to certain sections of the British and American secret services. The covert circumstances surrounding the devastating attack on America's main Pacific base have been reliably established and extensively written about over the years. The overwhelming body of published evidence about the attack is now well documented, but still worth recounting:

British military intelligence had known of Japan's hostile intention at least four months before the attack on Pearl Harbor. Dusko Popov, a Yugoslavian-born spy working for British intelligence, had provided forewarning which went disregarded. As Popov later disclosed in his memoirs, key British intelligence officers to whom he conveyed information derived from Japanese diplomatic circles did nothing to prevent the disaster.[14] Popov was not Britain's only source of intelligence about Japan's intentions. An Australian Navy cryptographer, Lieutenant Commander Eric Nave, working with the British Royal Navy's secret radio interception and code-breaking agency in Singapore, had deciphered a Japanese radio message sent on 19 November which indicated Japan was about to declare war against the United States. By 25 November further intercepts made it clear a large Japanese task force was at sea, with the intention of commencing hostilities, and that one of the most likely targets was Pearl Harbor.[15] Churchill, alerted by his own signals intelligence facilities and from all over the world, made sure none of this intelligence reached Roosevelt. The attack on Pearl Harbor, as Churchill later described it, was "a blessing" which brought America into the war. "Greater good fortune has rarely happened to the British Empire than this event."[16]

The withholding by Churchill of vital intelligence from the American leadership regarding the impending attack may well have been intended to ensnare the US in war against the Axis. If so, Churchill would apparently have been unaware the US Navy's own intercept station in Seattle had itself secretly decoded Japanese signals announcing imminent hostilities against the US. Journalist Robert Stinnert, in his book *Day of Deceit* contends that Roosevelt and his top advisors not only knew about the Japanese "sneak" attack, but actually caused it to happen in order to push the American people into the war. In October 1940, more than a year before the attack finally took place, Roosevelt had adopted a specific strategy to incite Japan to commit an overt act of war against the United States. Part of the strategy was to move America's Pacific fleet out of California and anchor it in Pearl Harbor. Admiral James Richardson, the commander of the

Pacific fleet, strongly opposed keeping the ships in harm's way in Hawaii. He expressed this to Roosevelt who promptly relieved him of his command.[17]

US cryptographers had in fact broken the all-important Japanese naval code JN-25 long before the attack on Pearl Harbor. The decrypted intercepts of Japanese radio messages had combined with radio direction findings to enable the Administration to know not only when the attack would come but where the attacking Japanese fleet was located. The standard histories of World War II hold that the US had *not* cracked the Japanese codes except for the diplomatic "Purple" code before Pearl Harbor and that, in the weeks before the attack, US intelligence had "lost track" of the Japanese fleet.

Official US naval records unearthed by Stinnert and by other researchers, however, show without question that from 17 to 25 November, the United States Navy intercepted and decoded numerous radio messages sent by Japan's Admiral Yamamoto to the task force of Japanese aircraft carriers preparing to attack Pearl Harbor. On 25 November 1941, Yamamoto sent a message that read: "… the task force, keeping its movements strictly secret and maintaining close guard against submarines and aircraft, shall advance into Hawaiian waters, and upon the very opening of hostilities shall attack the main force of the United States fleet in Hawaii and deal it a mortal blow …"[18] The US Chief of Staff then sent a coded message to Lieutenant-General Walter C Short, commander of the US Army's Hawaiian Department, warning of impending hostilities and ordering: "If hostilities cannot, repeat cannot, be avoided the United States desires that Japan commit the first overt act … Measures should be carried so as not, repeat not, to alarm civil population or disclose intent."[19]

When the attack on Pearl Harbor did come, it had the predictable effect of shocking the world and unifying American public opinion which had until then been sharply split between the isolationists, who resisted the prospect of being drawn into the war, and interventionists, who wanted to abandon neutrality. The isolationists recalled that in 1933 Britain had defaulted on the repayment of $4.7-billion in war debts to the US. This had been one of the obstacles to American financial reconstruction after the crash of Wall Street and the depression years that followed. Many disillusioned and recession-hit Americans supporting isolationism concluded that their country's participation in World War I had been a serious mistake.

German propagandists in pre-war America were aware of the political opportunities offered by the isolationist tendency and made repeated attempts to reinforce a neutral stance on the part of the American people. Through its embassy in America the Nazi government gave massive financial support to an open advertising campaign and to the bribery of selected American journalists for the purpose of encouraging a neutralist stance stressing the folly of war and wisdom of pacifism.[20] American novelist and World War 1 veteran Ernest Hemingway, by contrast, had no need of bribery to induce him to write in 1935:

> Of the hell broth that is brewing in Europe we have no need to drink. Europe has always fought: the intervals of peace are only armistices. We were fools to be sucked in once in a European war, and we shall never be sucked in again."[21]

When the Japanese attacked Pearl Harbor, most Americans did not even known where Pearl Harbor was; many of those who knew it was in far-off Hawaii thought it had nothing to do with America. The recently appointed intelligence chief Colonel William Donovan, promptly took care of that. Donovan, who was also responsible for the Office of War Information, dispatched bulletins to the editors of all major news publications, emphasising that Pearl Harbor was definitely part of the US and hence America itself had been attacked. The American public was left in no doubt that Pearl Harbor was an American port and American ships had been sunk. This immediately mobilised public consensus in favour of catapulting America into World War II.

The public mood henceforth allowed the Roosevelt administration and Congress to take concrete steps toward entry into the war while avoiding public discussion that would otherwise have been set off by a Senate debate over any proposed declaration of war. This would permit the spending, without public accountability or fiscal restraint, of hitherto unprecedented amounts of public monies on manufacturing armaments, and the research and development of secret weapons including the atomic bombs that would ultimately be dropped on Japan. It was of course not known generally, both then as now, that no attempt had been made to prevent, repel or at least minimise the devastating effects of Japan's attack on Pearl Harbor. Nor was it publicly recognised that the lack of preparedness at Pearl Harbor inferred a desire on the part of America's central war planners to be so attacked.

The fact that both the British and the American secret services had broken the Japanese naval code JN-25 was deemed so secret that for 50 years both the United States and the United Kingdom would deny it. Similarly, written correspondence between Churchill and Roosevelt at around the time of Pearl Harbor would disappear completely from official files and archives. Should those documents ever be found, however, they may confirm the substance of a momentous agreement concluded secretly between Britain and America just a few hours *before* the "surprise" attack on Pearl Harbor. As later disclosed by nuclear physicist Robert Jungk, a key scientist in the atomic bomb project, this secret agreement was that America would finance and forthwith expand vastly the development of an atomic bomb in collaboration with Britain.[22]

Chapter 2:

Singapore

On the day that Japan attacked Pearl Harbor, Japanese troops started invading the British colony of Malaya — Britain having been at war with Japan since October the previous year. As with the by now familiar pattern of "intelligence failures" as occurred at Pearl Harbor and at Coventry before, the invasion of Malaya did not come as any bolt from the blue. Churchill and his advisers had for a long time been well appraised of the vulnerability of Singapore, the key naval base at the southern tip of Malaya. Britain's Chief of Imperial General Staff, Field-Marshal Sir John Dill, had warned fully six months earlier that Singapore's defences were considerably below standard. If Britain waited until an emergency arose in the Far East before improving those defences, Dill stressed, it would be "too late".[1]

His warning went apparently disregarded while the military leadership at Singapore induced a state of general ill-preparedness and non-resistance. Vital available intelligence and other information warning of a concerted attack was either suppressed or ignored deliberately. This conformed in all major aspects with the patterned distribution of circumstances leading up to the debacle at Pearl Harbor.

Major-General S Woodburn Kirby, a veteran of the Far East theatre of operations, and other Far East specialists, have published credible accounts of the events leading up to the fall of Singapore. Some of their main observations are worth recounting. On 7 December, the day of the attack on Pearl Harbor, unopposed

Japanese forces swiftly established a beach-head in northern Malaya, captured three important RAF airfields and began sweeping southwards towards Singapore.[2] Shortly before the invasion of northern Malaya began, Reuters news agency had reported the sighting of Japanese transport ships off the southern tip of Indo-China. When this news was published in Singapore's *Malaya Tribune*, its editor was swiftly castigated by the Commander-in-Chief of the Far East, Air Chief Marshall Sir Robert Brooke-Popham, who complained: "I consider it most improper to print such alarmist views at a time like the present ... the position isn't half so serious as the *Tribune* makes out."[3] This came reassuringly at a time when Pearl Harbor and most of the American fleet in the Pacific had just been wiped out, and the same fate now threatened Singapore.

On 8 December, the day after Pearl Harbor and with the Japanese invasion of mainland Malaya now well under way, Brooke-Popham issued a public communiqué claiming that the Japanese had failed in an attempt to land in force. "All (Japanese) surface craft are retiring at high speed", the communiqué boasted, "and the few (Japanese) troops left on the beach are being heavily machine-gunned."[4] In no way did this statement correspond with reality, nor could it have been intended to deceive the invaders. The Japanese knew perfectly well they had already captured three important RAF airfields in northern Malaya and were currently sweeping southwards toward Singapore. The defenders of Singapore were therefore the only possible targets of Brooke-Popham's lies.

Churchill had by this time dispatched to the island his special envoy and close personal friend Duff Cooper who now became the newly appointed President of the War Council on Singapore. Cooper, a former British Information Minister, had earlier been involved in a tenacious fight to secure control of SO1 — the deception, subversive propaganda and psychological warfare department of the Special Operations Executive (SOE). After the war nearly all official documentation concerning this exceptionally secret organisation would be destroyed, making it impossible for future historians to analyse and evaluate properly SOE's wartime activities.

What is known, however, is that SOE operated entirely independently of the War Office and represented a third arm of the secret services — the other two being MI5 and MI6, responsible respectively for domestic security and foreign espionage. SOE was engaged specifically in carrying out absolutely secret, irregular operations funded by unvouchered monies outside parliamentary control.[5]

Once installed on Singapore Island, Cooper had considered it an important part of his new duties to present Singaporeans with a generally distorted picture of the deteriorating battle situation on the mainland, the rapid rate of enemy advance, and the disaster that was about to descend on them. Broadcasting on the government-controlled airwaves of the Malaya Broadcasting Corporation, Cooper deliberately misled Singaporeans at a time when Britain's strategic mainland base of Penang had already fallen to the Japanese. News of the debacle was delayed until fully three days after the event, being announced officially only when defeat on the mainland could no longer be concealed credibly: when refugees from the mainland began staggering into Singapore.[6]

When the first Japanese air raid was launched against the island, Air Vice-Marshal Sir Paul Maltby had a clear 30 minutes warning of approaching enemy aircraft, yet no RAF interceptors were dispatched nor was any public air raid alert given. When he complained about the absence of suitable shelters, one divisional air raid precaution commander was told the military leadership that such complaints "struck a serious blow to public morale".[7] That hundreds of civilians were now dying in sustained Japanese air attacks apparently had little to do with morale.

Some journalists at Singapore, for their part, had long been concerned about the visible lack of adequate defences, but for months they were prevented by vigorous censorship from warning

Singaporeans properly about the island's dangerous lack of preparedness in the face of approaching catastrophe. Not only were most Singaporeans kept in total ignorance about critical developments on the war front which concerned them directly but the military censors saw to it that even people back in Britain were kept effectively in the dark about those developments. The approved role of journalists was seen by the censors as one of parroting unquestioningly government handouts similar to the one published by the *Malaya Tribune* on 9 December 1941:

> We are ready. We have had plenty of warning and our preparations are made and tested ... we are confident. Our defences are strong and our weapons efficient ... we have one aim and one only, it is to defend these shores, to destroy such of our enemies as may set foot on our soil ... What of the enemy? We see before us a Japan drained for years by the exhausting claims of her wanton onslaught on China ... Let us all remember that we here in the Far East form part of the great campaign in the world of truth and justice and freedom.[8]

General Sir Archibald Wavell, Commander-in-Chief of American, British, Dutch and Australian forces in the Far East had in the mean time ordered specifically that no work be undertaken on preparing the island's defences. Wavell had a year earlier been a founder of Britain's strategic deception service, which had its pre-war origins in Palestine, where Wavell had energetically commanded British forces in 1936.[9]

His ostensible inertia over the threat to Singapore in February 1942 came to an end only when the enemy started openly to mass for a final assault. Only then were minimal, wholly inadequate defences hurriedly and chaotically prepared under the direction of General Sir Arthur Percival, the General Officer Commanding Malaya.[10]

In London, Churchill at last issued a clarion call to arms in late January 1942, two months after the first clear signs of an impending Japanese onslaught. By this time Singapore, Britain's "impregnable fortress", had already commenced its slide over the edge of disaster. Only now did Churchill, in a rare and belated display of forthrightness, inform the British Parliament: "There has been bad news lately from the Far East, and I think it highly probable ... we shall have a great deal more".[11]

This was fully a year after Britain had set up a special codebreaking unit on the island where it was secretly intercepting, decoding and analysing Japanese ciphers inclu-ding the earlier warnings of the impending attack on Pearl Harbor. The Americans were by this time also conveying to Britain all decoded intercepts of Japanese radio commun-ications monitored from America.[12] As later disclosed by the head of the US Navy's codebreakers, Commander Laurence F Safford, there was "authentic, timely and complete information concerning ... the mobilisation and movements of Japanese amphibious forces for the conquest of Southeast Asia".

This valuable information included "minute details of Japanese movements towards Singapore".[13] Yet virtually nothing had been done to secure the safety of Singapore. In fact the very opposite was true. When the Japanese launched their amphibious assault against Singapore on 8 February 1942, General Percival specifically ordered British artillery units not to fire at General Yamashita's advanced command headquarters and main observation point which was visible clearly, just a mile away across the Straits of Jahore. When the order was given eventually to open fire on the Japanese invaders, defending Australian shore batteries failed to receive the order. Someone had cut communications lines between them and their battle commanders.[14]

The die was cast. The "impregnable fortress" of Singapore, Britain's last and strongest foothold in the Far East, was overrun by numerically inferior forces and it surrendered on 8 February. The occupation force declared the island the capital of Japan's southern region and renamed it *Shonan*, meaning "Light of the South" in Japanese. More than 90,000 British, Australian and Indian troops were condemned to spend the next three years in misery as Japanese prisoners of war. Total British, Australian, Indian and volunteer manpower lost as a result of battle casualties in Malaya and by the surrender of Singapore amounted to 138,708.[15] They and the world at large were unaware the disaster that befell the island was largely avoidable.

Singapore's visible lack of preparedness and the rapidity of its unconditional surrender probably came as more of a surprise to the Japanese than to anyone else. General Yamashita, commander of the Japanese 25th Army, recorded in his diary that his invading force had by that time almost completely run out of ammunition and was outnumbered by more than three to one. In Yamashita's own words, the attack on Singapore was "a bluff". [16] A determined counter-offensive at that point would have stopped the invaders in their tracks.

Duff Cooper, Churchill's special envoy, had by then abandoned both his soothing public assurances and Singapore itself, fleeing safely to London before the garrison surrendered. A Royal Commission investigation promised by Churchill into the fall of Singapore simply failed to materialise. Overall blame for the fiasco was deftly shifted by Churchill onto the shoulders of the hapless Sir Shenton Thomas, Governor of Singapore at the time of its surrender. Sir Shenton, when he was eventually released from Japanese internment after the war, would nobly refrain from writing an autobiography because "too many heads would roll".[17] Others were less accommodating: In an angry protest cabled to Churchill, the Australian government described the fall of Singapore as "an inexcusable betrayal".[18] Whatever the truth of this "inexcusable betrayal", it is certainly the case that here began one of the cruellest military occupations in modern times.

To this day the British Foreign Office refuses to say why official documents in the key 1941 Japan files at the Public Record Office remain closed to public scrutiny until the year 2016. Even then the embargo may be further extended, and we might never know for certain why this strategic naval base, which had cost £60-million and taken 17 years to build, was jettisoned without even a proper fight. In the meantime, the few official documents that have been made available are bland and serve some official purpose which, whatever it may be, is clearly not for the irrelevant purpose of informing historians.

Much new material has, however, become available in recent years through the publication of memoirs by participants and former Japanese soldiers, and through the systematic efforts of the history and Asian studies departments at the universities of Nanzan and Waseda, in Japan. They have accumulated and archived a large number of oral histories and Chinese-language materials that provide some clues and a unique perspective on the "inexplicable" surrender of Singapore and the events that followed.

A systematic purge of Singapore's ethnic Chinese population was launched. An estimated 50,000 lost their lives. About 600 Malay and 45,000 Indian troops were assembled by the Japanese and urged to transfer their allegiance to the emperor of Japan. Many refused and were executed, tortured, imprisoned, or sent as forced labourers to Thailand, Sumatra, or New Guinea. Large numbers of Indian and Australian soldiers taken prisoner of war would die, some from summary execution by beheading, many others from diseases like beri-beri, malaria, diphtheria, dysentery and cholera.

Many prisoners were shipped north to Thailand to work on construction of the notorious Burma Railroad where, undernourished and maltreated, many were literally worked to death. Others were sent to Japan and some of these died when the freighters they were being transported on were sunk by American submarines.[19]

In Singapore itself, the Japanese secret police or *Kempeitai*, not unlike the Gestapo in occupied Europe, responded ruthlessly to any sign of resistance. They rounded up, tortured and interrogated all those suspected to be communists or communist sympathisers — meaning those pointed out by informers or who simply happened to be teachers, journalists or intellectuals. Some were imprisoned, but an estimated 25,000 were massacred, including the entire top layer of the Malayan communist leadership on the island — about 90 people in all.[20]

The Malayan Communist Party (MCP) had been active since 1928 in Malaya and it formed a party in Singapore in 1930. But it was an underground movement and many of its members had been jailed by the colonial police. When the war began Southeast Asia's communists had taken the general Marxist view and tried to ignore it, claiming that it was a war between imperialists, which did not concern them.[*] That point of view changed in 1940-41, because of Japan's alliance with Germany, followed by Germany's invasion of the Soviet Union. Now the war became a struggle to defend communism, and communists everywhere including the MCP declared war against the Axis powers.[21]

On 8th December 1941, after the Japanese had landed at Kota Bahru on the mainland, the MCP offered to fight on the side of the British Forces in Malaya in return for British arms and a promise of post-war independence from British colonial rule. Sir Shenton Thomas, the Governor of Singapore, rejected this offer by MCP leader Chin Peng and his Plenipotentiary. On 18th December when the situation worsened in northern Malaya, the MCP repeated its offer and this was accepted.[22] Britain and America had by this time signed the 1941 Atlantic Charter which

---

* As a counter to communist ideological influence on the MPAJA, SOE later established 'Force 136' consisting of guerilas more likely to favour nationalist Chinese leader Chiang Kai Chek.

lured thousands of indigenous people throughout the British Empire, and including Malaya, into the war against fascism in return for a British and American declaration of respect for "the right of all peoples to choose the form of government under which they will live".[23]

The Allied High Command released the MCP political leadership and militant communists jailed at Changi Prison, with SOE agreeing to train and arm them at 101 Special Training School in Tanjung Balai in Singapore, along with additional members recruited by the MCP.[24] The Malayan People's Anti-Japanese Army (MPAJA) thus came into being, comprising four battalions of about 4,000 combatants, primarily of ethnic Chinese origin and supported by tens of thousands of sympathisers among the rural peasantry. These resistance groups together with a handful of British military advisers and guerrilla warfare specialists were then hurriedly deployed on the mainland where they survived deep in the jungle, providing Britain with valuable intelligence about Japanese movements, and conducting high-risk sabotage operations and hit-and-run raids behind enemy lines.[25]

Meanwhile, from the comfort of their bureaucratic surroundings in London with splendid views of St James Park, the British colonial authorities had good reason to be appalled at the prospects of a coherent, communist-led post-war independence movement in the Far East..[26] But all that changed when America was catapulted into the war against Japan. Churchill, for one, would have known perfectly well that American participation in the secret atomic bomb project now tipped the balance of power completely in favour of the West.

The new correlation of forces in the Far East meant that the short term advantages offered to Britain by its communist allies in Malaya could now be subordinated to the long term threat posed by the MPAJA to Britain's post-war colonial interests. Accordingly, the fall of Singapore brought an abrupt discontinuation of British support for the MPAJA guerrillas. Supplies of arms and ammunition to the MPAJA, which would have been possible through clandestine air drops and submarine landings, ceased entirely.

This was much to the disappointment of the SOE military adviser Colonel Spencer Chapman, who was trapped in the jungle when the Allied High Command ordered his fellow British officers to withdraw after the surrender of Singapore. Chapman remained in the jungle for the duration of the Japanese occupation, and continued to advise the guerillas with whom he was on very friendly terms.[27] The MPAJA freedom fighters, against all odds, would later emerge from the war as heroes, and attempt to seize power from the British colonial authorities when Britain reneged on its promise to grant independence to Malaya in return for the MPAJA having fought the Japanese.[*]

Given the 75 years embargo placed by the British government on classified documents in the key 1941 Japan files at the Public Record Office, it is reasonable to assume that Churchill or the Allied High Command or the British Chiefs of Staff had something to hide. To this day there has not been any official explanation as to why Churchill jettisoned Singapore without even a proper fight, but the evidence points inescapably to one of the greatest betrayals in the history of military alliances. In all likelihood, the post-invasion massacre by the Japanese of the entire MCP political leadership accomplished what Churchill and the British colonial authorities secretly wanted, without having been able to act in such a way as to alienate Russia, Britain's only fighting ally in Europe at that time.

Apologists for Churchill and his cronies might argue that the criterion for right conduct is the overall value of its

---

[*] The leadership of the MPAJA then went underground, emerging again in 1948 to lead an armed uprising against British colonialism, which lasted several years before the nascent independence movement was crushed by a numerically superior British Commonwealth force including Rhodesians.

consequences – the principle that the end justifies the means. From this utilitarian standpoint, Britain's central war planners were behaving ethically; their decisions would in the long run benefit a majority of British people; their actions would lead to the greatest good of the greatest number.

This notion is whimsical, if not criminal. Ethics do not render human suffering an acceptable means for the achievement of long-term political goals. That gives rise to a conflict between morality and expediency, because the end justifies the means only within very narrow limits. Ethics are not merely a function of political utility but the very essence of what distinguishes civilisation from barbarism. The actions and decisions of Churchill and his elite cabal of advisers were in fact unscrupulous, opportunistic, and concerned only with the preservation of their class and the British Empire.

Those who did the actual fighting and dying, the untold numbers of Allied soldiers who were sacrificed on the altar of deception, were motivated by a belief in the war as an honourable crusade for humanity against Evil. They thought they were fighting and dying for a cause worth fighting and dying for — while the political elite lied unashamedly to the armed forces and to the public at large. Churchill and his backroom cabal implemented treacherous betrayals, and kept the media lying on their behalf, not in order to protect the "security of the nation" against the enemy, but to protect themselves against the probability of dissent if their real strategy became known. There would be further betrayals, as Stalin and the Red Army were about to discover in Europe.

Chapter 3:

Bomber Barons

The fall of Singapore, Britain's "impregnable fortress" in the Far East, served to strengthen an already prevalent belief in Britain that Allied forces were either in retreat or unavoidably confined to purely defensive action on every front and theatre of the war. British public opinion was misled to believe aerial bombardment offered the only means whereby offensive pressure of any kind could be brought to bear against Germany at that juncture of the war.

The public generally accepted this official explanation because, in the wake of Coventry, there was a knee-jerk tendency to support retaliation with whatever means available. It would have been a convenient frame of mind for Churchill to exploit, which probably accounts for the new directive that arrived at Bomber Command headquarters on 8 February 1941, the same day that Singapore surrendered. The directive, issued by the Air Ministry but bearing all hallmarks of Churchill and his closest advisers, authorized Bomber Command to employ its aircraft "without restriction" in raids upon selected German towns and cities. The fullest possible use of incendiary bombs was urged by Chief of the Air Staff, Sir Charles Portal, who specified aiming points to be "the built-up areas ... This must be made clear if not already understood".[1] Terror bombing thus became permissible in all but name.

German civilians had in fact been coming under bombardment by the RAF ever since the raid on Coventry three months earlier,[2] so the new directive that arrived at Bomber Command simply acceded officially to accomplished fact. What *was* innovative, was the introduction to the English language of a number of confusing new words and phrases, or new usage of existing ones. Some of these actually meant the very opposite of what they were supposed to imply. Terror bombing for instance was euphemistically referred to in public and in Parliament as "strategic bombing" or "area bombing" – without specifying that the areas at issue were in fact civilian residential areas. To have mentioned this would have been inconsistent with the stated values of a morally enlightened nation such as the British. It set a useful precedent for later linguistic developments when words such as "collateral damage" would accompany the gradual emergence of a whole new category of weapons of mass destruction including nuclear warheads, space-based laser weapons, and chemical and biological weapons. These would be referred to as "deterrents" when the West stockpiled them and "weapons of mass destruction" when any other side was suspected of doing so.

Back in the 1940s, meanwhile, the publicly stated objective of the "strategic air offensive" was to bring German war production to a halt.[3] This objective, on the face of it, may have been convincing to a beleaguered nation desperate for something, anything, upon which to pin its hopes for a speedy end to the war. In practice, by contrast, the halting of German war production would prove to be a deceptive and wholly unattainable objective. Public acceptance of the overtly stated objective was made possible only because an entire dimension was missing from the perceptions upon which people normally relied. The public, parliament, most of the Cabinet and the airmen of Bomber Command who risked their lives were not informed that, behind the scenes, certain exceptionally secret Anglo-American scientific experiments were gathering momentum for the production of neutron-induced radioactivity and nuclear fission. The ultimate outcome of these experiments would render obsolete the usually accepted norms of civilized behavior and alter irrevocably the methods of orthodox military strategy. "Conventional" aerial bombardment would be useful only as a "softening up" process in conditioning public opinion for the "big one".

A secret committee known as Maud had been formed in 1940, entrusted with planning and co-ordinating Britain's nuclear weapons program, which was placed under the Ministry of Aircraft Production — hence the acronym Maud, meaning Ministry of Aircraft (Production) and Uranium Development. A patent for the production of nuclear fission had in 1939 been secretly assigned to the Admiralty when Churchill was First Sea Lord, and Churchill still regarded the experiments to be very much "his" project. [4] In this he was enthusiastically guided by Professor FA Lindemann, better known as Lord Cherwell, Churchill's personal scientific adviser and in fact the grand architect of terror bombing. Lindemann saw it as "the one and only useful operation of the war".[5] Not only did Cherwell feature prominently in the secret Anglo-American nuclear weapons program already under way, but his special relationship with Churchill enabled him to by-pass the entire official machinery and deliver briefings directly to Churchill.[6] So came into being the early linkages between secrecy, the conditioning of public opinion, and the "legitimizing" of long-range terror bombing in anticipation of an eventual nuclear weapon with unprecedented potential for mass destruction.

The world was headed for a great deal of trouble as Churchill now surrounded himself behind the scenes with a ghoulish cabal of sycophants and advisers of his own choosing, accountable only to himself and including among their number several key figures sharing Churchill's proven abhorrence of communism. Propaganda and public information policy was in the hands of Information Minister Brendan Bracken, one of

Churchill's close personal friends and constant companions. Strategic deception and psychological warfare operations were entrusted to the newly formed Political Warfare Executive (PWE) headed by Robert Bruce Lockhart. His links with Churchill went back to the 1918 when they, together with Brigadier Sir Stewart Menzies who now headed Britain's secret intelligence service, had been pivotal figures in the Allied invasion of northern Russia.[7]

This secretive junta was effectively in control of Britain's central war effort without the strictures of accountability and oversight. On the overt plane, the Defense Committee of the War Cabinet sat almost every day to discuss the reports of the Military Co-ordination Committee and those of the Chiefs of Staff, and their conclusions or divergences were referred frequently to Cabinet.[8] The procedure appeared outwardly to reflect a process of collective responsibility; but in essence it amounted to little more than an elaborate charade. Its basic function in terms of Churchill's elective dictatorship was to preserve outward appearances while he got on with the covert business of running the war more-or-less single-handedly.

Few if any of the most important decisions affecting the war were actually being made by the War Cabinet's defense committee, which was supposedly responsible for directing the national war effort. The committee had little real influence in determining the course of action and frequent inaction upon which Churchill was embarked, representing political activity on two separate but interrelated planes — one plane democratically invested, the other autocratically executed. The collegiate nature of Cabinet government was fatally weakened, and the power of Churchill and his secret team would grow at its expense. A similar situation existed on the other side of the Atlantic where, with the power of veto on grounds of "military security", only one man in the War Department, General Leslie Groves, was in effect determining and virtually running foreign policy on his own — without the knowledge even of the Department of State.[9]

Beyond Groves, Roosevelt and his own secret cabal, however, Churchill's enthusiasm for irregular methods of governance won him few friends. Britain's Secretary for War, Anthony Eden, soon became "very fed up" with Churchill's "monopolistic tendencies".[10] Lord Salisbury, a leading conservative in the House of Lords urged radical organizational changes to loosen Churchill's grip. "If we are not careful," Lord Salisbury warned Eden, "Winston will be in his grave or in a lunatic asylum".[11] Major-General Sir John Kennedy, Britain's official Director of Military Operations, observed that Churchill was by now wielding "constant bludgeon-strokes" on the daily work of the Chiefs of Staff while scarce resources were diverted away from the army and navy and channelled solely into the "strategic" air offensive against Germany.[12]

Kennedy, suggesting that 40 percent of the bomber effort be taken off Germany and distributed in the Middle East and elsewhere, considered it doubtful whether Rommel would even have started his North African offensive if only 20 percent of Britain's bomber force had been diverted to the Middle East in the first place. Tobruk was now threatened by Rommel's forces and its loss could result in the virtually unchallenged use by Germany of a prized North African seaport close to Britain's vital oil supply routes in the Middle East.[13]

Fierce contention also ensued between the Commander of the Imperial Chief of General Staff, Field-Marshal Sir Alan Brooke (later Lord Alanbrooke) and the Chief of Air Staff, Sir Charles Portal, on the issue of inadequate tactical air support for the British Army. The argument was settled by Churchill who ordered an intensification of the bombing campaign. [14]

The bombing campaign had earlier been approved and intended by the Chiefs of Staff as a precursor to an Allied invasion of occupied Europe which would force Germany to fight on two separate fronts simultaneously, dividing their main force and taking the brunt of the fighting off Soviet troops on the eastern front. The bombing of Germany, Churchill assured Stalin, was "to force Hitler to bring back some of his air power to the West and gradually take some of the strain off you."[15] The same message had been delivered to the British people by the Secretary of State for Air, Sir Archibald Sinclair. The objectives of the bombing campaign, Sinclair told the House of Commons, included a need "to relieve the pressure of the German Air Force and armies on our Russian allies".[16] The theme was faithfully taken up by the media and believed by the public; but as with the earlier claim that the bomber offensive was aimed at "halting German war production", this "support for Russia" would ultimately turn out to be a false pretext. More accurate and to the point were Churchill's words when he confided privately to the Defense Committee of the War Cabinet that, with Russia engaged in a desperate struggle against Germany, "every advantage which such a conflict offered" would be taken by Britain.[17]

Churchill began including a regular series of late-night get-togethers between himself and Bomber Command's commander-in-chief, Air Marshal Arthur "Bomber" Harris, at the Prime Minister's country retreat which was situated within easy distance of Bomber Command headquarters in High Wycombe. Here, without any strictures of oversight, Churchill and Harris privately formulated strategy and tactics, in effect enabling Churchill to maintain control of bomber operations while bypassing the Defence Committee of the War Cabinet. In this manner, and without the interference of what they saw as "rival interest groups", an unprecedented operation involving 1,000 bombers was secretly planned by Churchill and Harris. The maximum force concentrated previously against a single target in Germany had been a mere 228 bombers.[18]

Their plan was implemented in an operation codenamed "Millenium" taking place on the night of 30/31 May 1942 when an armada of 1,046 bombers took off from various British airfields, heading for Cologne in Germany, a city of nearly 300,000 people. When the smoke cleared the next day, aerial reconnaissance showed 600 acres devastated, half of them in the city centre. Nearly half a million people were made homeless with 469 killed and 5,027 injured.[19]

An analysis of private British letters examined by the British censors confirmed that "satisfaction" was the predominant response of British public opinion in the aftermath of Cologne.[20] The raid was probably a source of great personal satisfaction to Churchill as well. Not only did this single operation test the extent to which public opinion was tolerant of terror bombing, but the operation also served a useful purpose of distracting public attention from the avoidable defeats the British Army and its allies were then suffering in Burma and North Africa. Harris, after his private, late-night meetings with Churchill, had bluntly refused to deploy his bombers in the North African campaign. The South Africans were forced to rely on a handful of near-obsolete Boston bombers against superior numbers of German forces, resulting in the surrender of Tobruk on 21 June 1942 in an avoidable military debacle reminiscent of Singapore. Nearly 10,000 South African soldiers — one third of the entire South African force in the field – were condemned to spend the rest of the war as prisoners.[21] It was typical of the heavy price paid by Britain's colonial allies as a consequence of Churchill's hidden duplicity.

Nonetheless, whereas before the raid on Cologne it had seemed as if Britain was either in retreat or confined to purely defensive action on every front and theatre of the war, after the destruction of Cologne things were perceived by the public as radically different. Britain now appeared to possess an immensely powerful weapon that could provide the kind of initiative that comes only from being on the offensive. Not much was said officially about the many airmen – mostly novices fresh out of

flying school — who failed to return from the Cologne raid.[22]
Churchill, secure in the knowledge that he had won the necessary
public consensus upon which to base the "legitimacy" of terror
bombing, announced that the Cologne raid was "the herald of
what Germany will receive, city by city, from now on". Harris
was congratulated by Churchill for his "remarkable feat".[23] Barely
two weeks later *The Times* announced that Harris had been
created a Knight Commander of the Bath. Sir Arthur celebrated
by ordering a further 1,000-bomber raid on Germany.[24]

Soon most British newspapers were voicing opinions
similar to that of the London *Daily Mail* when it assured readers
on 18 December 1942 that the large-scale bombing of Germany
was a "war-winning strategy" that was "paying good dividends".
Public support for the escalating bomber offensive was
reaffirmed by a Mass Observation survey showing six out of 10
Londoners approved of British raids on German towns and cities
"without qualification."[25]

The Americans, similarly impressed by Harris's
"remarkable feat", agreed to a continuation of the air offensive
against Germany with as many new American-supplied heavy
bombers as possible, manned by British crews. The supply of
these aircraft, like other American war material then pouring into
Britain was not, however, based on selfless altruism. The price
Britain paid for American supplies of war material was very high
and included surrendering Britain's rights and royalties in various
achievements such as radar, antibiotics, jet aircraft and advances
in nuclear research. In all these fields America lagged far behind
Britain. Whereas the United States Army Air Force had never
even carried radar previously, it now gained immediate access to
the resonant magnetron, a new device that tremendously
increased radar power and placed the Allies far in advance of
corresponding German technology for the remainder of the
war.[26]

Britain's down-payment for help from across the

Atlantic further included the surrender of some of its foreign markets, and Britain would thus emerge ultimately from the war as the world's largest debtor nation. Only the United States would become richer, much richer because of the war, which provided the American economy with a great boost to growth, taking the country from virtual recession to decisive world economic leadership. During the period 1940 to 1944 domestic American industrial expansion was to rise by 15 percent — a faster pace than at any period before or since. War production soared from 2 percent of total output in 1939 to 40 percent in 1943.[27]

In Britain, capital expenditure on the RAF by early 1943 leaped far ahead of both the Army and Navy. In the words of Sir John Grigg, the Army Minister, it was an "extraordinary situation in which the labour devoted to the production of heavy bombers alone is believed to be equal to that allotted to the production of the whole equipment of the army."[28]

The costs to Britain and America of their combined air offensive against Germany were enormous too in terms of human lives. The British-based US Army Air Force, once it began venturing into Germany on deep-penetration daylight raids against military targets, lost as many as 4,700 aircraft in just a few months — the average life of a Flying Fortress bomber was estimated to be just 160 days.[29] On its night-time and hence less dangerous raids, RAF Bomber Command also took heavy casualties. Between the two air forces, their combined losses would amount to nearly 100,000 men killed by the time war ended.[30]

Yet, despite official British attempts to suppress their findings, independent British and American post-war surveys would prove the bombing of Germany was conducted on the basis of official claims far in excess of the facts. Although nearly half a million German civilians, their dwellings and possessions were destroyed, the bombing in fact had very little effect on

German armaments production or on the German people's general commitment to the war.

The bombing of Germany was in fact an extravagant failure. The production of German fighter aircraft in particular was unaffected, nor was the morale of the German people broken or even significantly impaired by the bombing. As the independent British Bombing Survey Unit (BBSU) bluntly expressed it: "The essential premise behind the policy of treating towns as unit targets for area attack, namely that the German economic system was fully extended, was false." This, the BBSU noted, was because official estimates of German war production were "more than 100 percent in excess of the true figures". The BBSU concluded: "Far from there being any evidence of a cumulative effect on (German) war production, it is evident that, as the (bombing) offensive progressed ... the effect on war production became progressively smaller (and) did not reach significant dimensions." Contrary to Churchill's repeated claim that the Allied bomber offensive was aimed at relieving pressure on the Russian-German front, and "the most potent method of impairing the enemy's morale", the will of the German people was actually strengthened by the aerial bombardment.[31]

Far from the bombing of Germany being of any help to the Russians, as publicly claimed by Churchill, the very opposite was true. In the absence of British and American ground or air support for the Red Army on the eastern front, the key Russian cities of Leningrad and Stalingrad were being pounded by the *Luftwaffe* and besieged by the German army. In Stalingrad alone two million civilians were dying from the German air attacks, while German armour rapidly advanced in an encircling movement aimed at Moscow.[32]

It is inconceivable that Churchill and the Allied intelligence services were unaware of the true situation on the ground, both in Germany and in Russia. Apart from intelligence derived from Ultra, and from aerial photo reconnaissance and agents in the field, the

Western Allies were receiving top-secret military and political intelligence reports supplied clandestinely by a group of very senior German officers known as the *Schwarze Kapelle*, who were vigorously opposed to Hitler and Nazism. These rebellious German officers — among them Admiral Wilhelm Canaris, chief of the German secret intelligence service — were providing Churchill with information of vital significance about the Third Reich's most important secrets. At great risk to themselves, it was the intention of the *Schwarze Kapelle* to bring an early end to the war, and to gain Western support and win concessions favourable to Germany once it was rid of Hitler and the Nazis. *

All of this invites a critical assessment of prevailing notions about what the Western military and political leadership intended, compared with what they did in fact achieve through feeding lies to the public about the otherwise senseless bombing of Germany. An inescapable conclusion is that Churchill and his accomplices were not intent on ending the war, but on actually prolonging it, and thereby allowing Hitler time to bring his full force to bear on the Russians.

A purposeful prolongation of the war would also allow the foundations to be laid for the development of air-atomic strategy — a graduated threat-system directed against a war-weakened Soviet Union in the "post-war" years. The requirements of the military establishment were being welded to the productive capacities of private monopoly corporations under the aegis of government, while weapons production and procurement programs became thoroughly intrinsic to the subversion of

---

* Among other things, the *Schwarze Kapelle* or "Black Orchestra" attempted unsuccessfully on several occasions to assassinate Hitler. [The history of the *Schwarze Kapelle* is documented in: Walter Schellenberg, *The Schellenberg Memoirs*, London: Deutsch, 1956; Habian von Schlabrendorff, *The Secret War Against Hitler*, London: Hodder & Stoughton, 1966; John Wheeler-Bennett, *The Nemesis of Power: The German Army in Politics*, London: Macmillan, 1953].

democracy, including the manipulation of public opinion. Weapons procurement was profitably fusing into one entity the productive capacity of private enterprise and the destructive capacity of strategic air power. The mass production of long-range strategic bombers in particular would foster an ever-increasing band of private companies, cementing into a solid bloc the defense departments of the main Western powers, their strategic planners, and private enterprise.[33] Giant corporations such as McDonnel Douglas and General Electric would remain the main beneficiaries of a military-industrial system founded on public subsidy and producing private profit under the banner of "free market economy".

At the same time, a core public attitude was being forged upon which to base the "legitimacy" of terror bombing, which would ultimately have its enunciation at Hiroshima and Nagasaki in the single worst acts of savagery ever known to humankind.

Chapter 4:

The Missing Front

Britain's Joint Intelligence Committee deemed it "imperative" at the end of the war that historians be prohibited from prying into "apparently unaccountable operational orders" carried out by the Western armed forces.[1] The result, to this day, is enduring public ignorance and mass mystification in the West concerning Britain and America's wartime alliance with the Soviet Union. It is clear, nonetheless, that something large and still largely suppressed was secretly going on behind the scenes. With the benefit of hindsight and the huge body of evidence assembled over the years by researchers, one may plausibly conjecture that the fight against Hitler was secretly subordinated by Churchill to an intense dislike of communism. This outweighed by far any real commitment by Churchill to the overt war against Nazism.

By land, sea and air, the Western Allies generally failed to deploy their overwhelming military advantages to good effect while Russia suffered appalling losses as a result. With Leningrad and Sebastopol in ruins and Stalingrad under siege, 10,000 Russians were dying every day in the greatest battle in the history of the world — the Russian-German war on the eastern front. Stalin probably had a valid point when he complained that British policy appeared to be "aimed at encouraging Germany and Russia to weaken and exhaust one another; and then, when they have become weak enough, to appear on the scene with fresh strength, to appear of course, in the 'interests of peace', and to dictate conditions to the enfeebled belligerent."[2]

The Red Army, engaging about four-fifths of Hitler's forces on the eastern front, was in a such a desperate situation in mid-1942 that Hitler bragged to his commanders that the Red Army was "as good as beaten".[3] This was no idle boast, and it would almost certainly have been picked up by Churchill through Ultra intercepts and decrypts. Still, there was no sign of the Western Allies relieving pressure on the Russians by opening a second front in Europe. In secret correspondence with Churchill, which would be made public by the Russians after the war, Stalin bluntly told Churchill on July 18, 1942 that their alliance had taken "an improper turn".

Churchill tried unconvincingly to defend his position by arguing there were nine German divisions in France, making it impossible for the Western Allies to launch a concerted ground offensive in western Europe. Stalin countered with the observation that there was "not a single German division in France of any (fighting) value" [4] This was corroborated later in classified German documents captured by the Allies, showing that the stationing of German troops in the campaign against Russia on the eastern front generally precluded effective defence in the west. In Hitler's own words, a major Allied landing in western Europe in mid-1942 would have brought the Germans "to a generally critical position". It would have drawn off an appreciable share of Hitler's forces from the Russian-German front, making it possible for the Red Army to deal a decisive blow which would either have crushed Germany immediately or made certain its defeat within a reasonably short period.[5] The inescapable conclusion to be drawn from this is that Churchill was not only loath to do anything to assist the Russians, but his actions and omissions were in effect actually prolonging the war.

The fragility of Russia's survival in mid-1942 was exacerbated by Churchill's mishandling of the German U-boat menace, at that time preventing essential war materials from being transported by Allied convoys across the Atlantic, then through the Arctic and round the northern tip of Norway to the north Russian ports of Murmansk and Archangel. These supplies had been promised to Russia by Roosevelt in terms of America's then recently legislated Lend-Lease Act; the Russians being desperate that the supplies should reach them in time to launch a concerted counter-offensive against the Germans on the principal and decisive front of the war.

There was, however, absolute resistance on the part of Churchill and the Air Staff to deploying very long-range aircraft to locate and attack both the U-boats and the auxiliary surface supply vessels upon which the U-boats were dependent. About 3,000,000 tonnes of Allied merchant shipping was consequently lost on the Atlantic and Arctic routes in the first six months of 1942 alone.[6] This huge loss could have been avoided, and the U-boat menace overcome, through the operational use by Bomber Command of very long-range anti-submarine aircraft capable of patrolling far into the Atlantic. These very long range aircraft had the capability of patrolling an area 1,100 miles from base for up to three hours at a time, using the RAF's highly advanced electronic surveillance and radio direction-finding equipment to locate the enemy with great accuracy. RAF Bomber Command had such aircraft, of which the Mark I Consolidated Liberators were the most impressive with an operational range of 2,400 miles, but Harris refused adamantly to deploy them on anti-submarine duties.[7]

In addition to the large tonnage of Allied shipping lost to U-boats in the Atlantic, the courageous convoys to northern Russia, if they actually managed to survive the perilous Atlantic crossing, faced further appalling hazards. They were being picked off by Germany's powerful surface squadron dominated by the battlecruiser *Scharnhorst* positioned in northern Norway. Astonishingly, the *Scharnhorst* had in February 1942 been allowed by Churchill's idiosyncratic style of war management to make a dash from the French port of Brest to Germany through British home waters. The episode caused *The Times* to declare on 17 February: "No more mortifying an episode has occurred in 300 years of British seapower". Against this background of events, Arctic convoy PQ13 which made passage at the end of March, lost five ships out of 20. PQ16, the May convoy, lost eight of the 35 that set out. The next convoy, PQ17, was almost a total disaster, losing 23 of its 34 ships as it struggled to reach Archangel. When it finally limped into port, no more than 70,000 tonnes of the convoy's original 200,000 tonnes of cargo had managed to reach destination.[8] Churchill used this, the largest maritime loss of the war, to justify his suspension of the convoys to Russia. They were "too dangerous" and to attempt further Arctic convoys at that time, he told Stalin, "would bring no benefit to you and would only involve a dead loss to the common cause". Stalin replied: "No major task can be carried out in wartime without risk or losses. You know of course that the Soviet Union is suffering far greater losses."[9]

Churchill persisted in claiming that aerial bombardment of Germany was a more effective method of taking pressure off the Russians than the opening of a second front in Europe. Yet potentially war-winning weapons systems allowing greatly improved precision bombing capability were either discouraged or withheld deliberately from operational use because they were "too valuable to risk over enemy territory".[10] Despite stiff opposition from the air force, the Miscellaneous Weapons Development Department of the Royal Navy, almost in desperation at the RAF's lack of co-operation, developed two types of remarkably accurate rocket-boosted and radar-guided flying bombs that could achieve direct hits on difficult targets from a safe height of 20,000 feet.[11]

Britain also had a wide margin of technological superiority over German radar, navigation and weapons delivery systems including guided missiles and advanced aiming systems.[12] There is no record of Churchill ever having considered sharing these secret weapons with Russia, and the same is true with regard to Ultra, the most secret weapon of all.

Some of these highly advanced weapons would either be deployed far too late in World War II to make any significant contribution to its outcome, or be deployed in such small numbers as to be insignificant, or not be deployed at all. This applied especially to fast tactical fighter-bombers such the RAF's Hawker Typhoon and the Mosquito, and also the American Mustang and P-47 Thunderbolt, which had the capability to conduct very precise attacks on enemy rail communications and troop movements deep in German territory. The RAF's Mosquito in particular, with the range of a bomber and the speed of a fighter, had the ability to carry a 4,000lb bomb while retaining a high survivability rate. With a super-charged top speed of 350 mph, it was faster than anything then available to the Germans. Its major advantage, as with all fighter-bombers, lay in the elements of precision and surprise, and many airmen were of the opinion these aircraft could win the war on their own if they were deployed in sufficient numbers. Several Mosquitoes could be built for the price of one heavy Lancaster bomber; yet production of Mosquitoes remained a low priority throughout the war, accounting for barely 10 percent of overall aircraft production.[13]

In short, aside from the huge intelligence advantages provided by Ultra, there was at Churchill's disposal a vast array of potentially war-winning weaponry, which he could have deployed had he been committed to shortening the war in Europe. That he failed to encourage the deployment of such weapons in sufficient quantity infers that Churchill intended deliberately to prolong the war, while the Red Army and the people of the Soviet Union continued to sustain huge losses in eastern Europe. The terms of warfare in Europe, while appearing to be those of Hitler, were in essence Churchill's terms, and they would remain so for the duration of World War II.

The ferocity and effectiveness of German air defences had meanwhile killed more members of the RAF than German civilians. Bomber Command had lost one aircraft for every 10 tonnes of bombs dropped. If shot down, aircrews had only a 20 percent chance of baling out and becoming prisoner. Of Bomber Command's casualties, more than 47,000 air crew would die on operations or in captivity before the war ended. Nearly 10,000 more would become prisoners and more than 8,000 would be wounded.[14] While Bomber Command was taking heavy casualties in 1942, German fighter aircraft production remained unscathed, forcing the heavy, lumbering RAF bombers to operate either from extreme altitude or by night. In the former case they could not hit any selected military targets, in the latter they could not even find their targets. Due to aiming difficulties they could hit nothing smaller than an entire German town.[15] Many aircrews missed their intended targets by up to five miles and more. As one British MP observed at the time: "As far as direct hits on specified industrial targets by high-flying aircraft by night are concerned, we might as well send the long-distance bombers to the moon."[16]

Only one leading British politician refused to be party to Churchill's manoeuvres. Lord Beaverbrook, when he resigned in mid-1942 as Minister for Supply, bluntly told the War Cabinet:

> I wish to take advantage of the rising temper in the country for helping Russia. Others don't. I want to make a supreme effort to raise production so as to help Russia. Others don't. I want to fulfil in every particular the agreement (to help Russia) made in Moscow. Others don't. The Chiefs of Staff don't. The line of cleavage between me and my colleagues and the Chiefs of Staff is complete.[17]

In response to Stalin's increasingly urgent pleas for the participation of British and American land forces in Europe, and to take the heat off Russia's diplomatic demands upon Britain, Churchill and Roosevelt had earlier assured Stalin a second front would definitely be formed in 1942. As the end of 1942 approached, with the Arctic convoys suspended due to heavy losses and with large numbers of American soldiers and equipment remaining idle in the British isles, Roosevelt was importuned by Soviet foreign affairs commissar Vyacheslav Molotov to "do something now". Roosevelt, forced to concede the hollowness of Churchill's earlier promises of opening a second front in Europe, warned his envoy in London that he was finally "going to insist on some action".[18]

Roosevelt's intervention ostensibly brought the temporising to an end, and an amphibious landing was staged in August 1942 at the German-held French port of Dieppe. The stated objective was, as usual, to provide relief to the Russians on the eastern front. Instead, it merely provided history with yet a further link in the disastrous chain of apparently inexplicable operational blunders that had come to characterise key moments of the war. Astonishingly, although plans for the invasion of France were supposed to be top-secret, and strict censorship of the media was in force, the BBC was encouraged to broadcast a warning to French citizens in the coastal regions of France that the Allied occupation of France was imminent. *The New York Times* repeated the BBC's announcement on June 9, 1942, bringing the Germans to a high state of preparedness and expectancy.

They had no difficulty surmising that Dieppe was the most likely landing spot. Although Ultra was providing Churchill with invaluable information about the strength and disposition of German troops in France, the by now familiar pattern reasserted itself. Vital available intelligence was either ignored, "inaccurately evaluated", or not communicated to the "invaders".[19] On August 19, the day of the landing, there was no preliminary bombardment; the operation was conducted in broad daylight;

usually reliable communications systems suddenly failed, and landing craft were specifically directed towards beaches that subsequently proved the least suitable for tanks. Those few tanks that did somehow manage to extricate themselves from the loose shingle soon found their advance blocked by anti-tank obstacles before the tanks were completely destroyed. Canadian troops forming the bulk of the landing force suffered enormous casualties: some of the Canadian regiments were virtually wiped out. Of 5,000 men from the Canadian 2nd Division, about 900 were killed and nearly 2,000 taken prisoner. The RAF lost 106 fighter planes, and more than 500 Royal Navy officers and ratings were killed, wounded, captured or missing. German casualties were a mere 600.[20]

On the face of it, the disaster at Dieppe represented a planning and intelligence failure of huge proportions — but "success" or "failure" in the shadowy world of strategic deception is largely a matter of human value judgement rather than any universally recognisable state. The hidden success of the operation lay in the fact that it effectively dispelled any hope of an early invasion by creating the illusion of a virtually invincible enemy force in western Europe. It provided Churchill with an apparently valid excuse for further inaction; he could plausibly deny that Britain was purposely dragging its heels in rendering assistance to the Russians at a time of their greatest need. He accordingly informed the Defence Committee of the War Cabinet that land operations in western Europe were out of the question. There was no chance of "doing anything on a scale likely to be of the slightest use" to Russia. [21]

This is perhaps what Churchill really meant when he recorded for posterity that "the results fully justified the heavy cost" of the disaster at Dieppe.[22] Only Admiral Lord Louis Mountbatten seems to have suspected something improper when he suggested to Admiral Ramsey that the Dieppe raid had been conducted "purely for political reasons".[23]

Much the same was occurring in the North African campaign against Rommel's panzer army, where seemingly inexplicable British armoured tactics and the deliberate withholding of adequate numbers of bomber aircraft from the desert campaign lent themselves well to German successes. The German armed forces, encouraged by the absence of RAF bombers which had earlier resulted in the surrender of 10,000 South African troops at Tobruk, continued to take major military risks in which they succeeded only because they were permitted to do so by Churchill and Britain's central war planners. Although Ultra was providing valuable information about the state of Rommel's fuel, ammunition and tank reserves, which were fast diminishing, German armour was on at least two occasions allowed to escape even though General Montgomery's 8th Army was in a ideal position to inflict crippling blows.

As one Ultra expert later described it: "Ultra was showing the British commanders a vision, but they let it vanish before their eyes like mist in the sun."[24] Hence Rommel's ability to regroup his panzer divisions for the defence of Tunisia after the German defeat at Alamein. This regrouping of the German panzer divisions caused Anglo-American operations in Tunisia to be suspended, allowing the Germans to quickly move 24 divisions, including five armoured divisions, from France and elsewhere to the Russian-German front.[25]

The Western media, meanwhile, presented the illusion of a happy, unclouded and fruitful relationship between Russia and West. So successful was the illusion that *Life* magazine in America devoted an entire edition to a laudatory description of the Soviet Union's accomplishments. It had already named Stalin as "Man of the Year" in 1941; now, in mid-1943 *Life* described Lenin as "perhaps the greatest man of modern times". In Britain, *The Times* simultaneously provided an admiring public with a comprehensive guide to Soviet affairs in the form of regular articles written by the historian EH Carr.[26]

The Western media's glowing admiration for the Soviet Union was apparently not shared by at least some elements of the American secret intelligence service. In February 1943 a group of them held secret talks in Switzerland with Prince Maximilian Hohenlohe, an agent of Himmler's SS. Their purpose, according to Soviet espionage reports, was to discuss the possibility of a separate peace between America and the Third Reich. Allen Dulles, the leader of the American delegation and later destined to head the American CIA, allegedly shared the Nazi vision of an undivided post-war Germany and the establishment of a *cordon sanitaire* against communism and Pan-Slavism.[27] The Nazis had long been pressing peace proposals on the Western Allies, in the hope that Germany could turn its undivided attention on the USSR. When Rudolf Hess had flown to Britain on May 10, 1941, he brought with him two specific peace proposals from Hitler: be neutral in a war between Germany and the Soviet Union, and Britain's Empire and spheres of interest would be guaranteed, or join Germany's assault on Russia, and Britain and Germany could then divide the spoils between them.[28]

Both offers were evidently rejected by Churchill, although to this day a veil of secrecy prevails in Britain over the Hess affair. Official British papers on the subject are officially withheld from the public domain, and the British Foreign Office refuses to say why – apart from the usual, bland nonsense about "national security" and the "national interest".

Even if the documents are ever released, the full story might still remain untold. As the historian Arnold Toynbee has noted:

> The information to be found in an official document will have been put there — if we may assume that the document has been drafted competently — in order to serve some official purpose which, whatever it may have been, will certainly not have been the irrelevant purpose of informing a future historian.[29]

What is clear, is that Churchill's obligation to open a second front in Europe was not honoured in 1943 and would remain unfulfilled for nearly another year while desperately needed aircraft and other essential supplies from the West failed to reach Stalin. The "strategic" bombing of Germany continued to derive false legitimacy from the core deception of "helping Russia" at a time when, behind the scenes, Cold War doctrine was being formulated by Churchill and his closest advisers. Public misperceptions were encouraged about Western support for the Russians when events on the battlefield and in the "strategic" air offensive against Germany were proving the very opposite to be true. Only Colonel Moore-Brabazon, Britain's Minister for Aircraft Production, may have had the honesty to admit the purpose behind Churchill's procrastination in opening a second front, when he boasted: "Let the German and Soviet armies tear into each other. We will pick up the pieces."[30]

Chapter 5:

The Lost Command

On the night of 24 July 1943 a new word came into being: "Firestorm". Never before had the world known anything like it. Over a period of just 10 days and nights, as great a number of British and American bombs fell on Hamburg, Germany's second largest city, as fell on London during the entire eight-months "blitz". For the architects of terror bombing Hamburg was a particularly attractive target. Bombs could fall as much as four miles short of the city centre without landing in open country, permitting the destruction of an area covering about three miles by one and a half — nearly all of it residential.

Of the many tonnes of bombs dropped on Hamburg, a high proportion consisted of incendiaries. The smaller of these lodged in roofs and attics, the larger ones plummeted through to start blazing fires inside buildings where heavy blast bombs blew in structures, doors and windows, scattering burning debris and creating strong draughts to spread the flames. The rising flames and the fumes in turn generated a whirlwind effect to fan the inferno while yet more incendiaries started fresh fires. Many people escaped into the open only to wither from the heat. By the time the last of the bombers departed, a wave of terror radiated from the stricken city where the rising smoke could be seen for days from a distance of 130 miles. One million people were left homeless.[1]

The destructive effects of a "conventional" firestorm were remarkably similar to those of a nuclear explosion. So it was

perhaps not entirely coincidental that the decision to bomb
Hamburg was taken on the very day that final work commenced
on assembling the first atomic bomb at the top-secret Los
Alamos laboratory site in New Mexico.[2] Certainly, the Hamburg
raid did not conform in any way with the primary objective of
official targeting policy which was stated publicly as "the
destruction of enemy fighters in the air and on the ground".[3] This
had been agreed jointly by the British and American leaders when
they and their closest military adviser had met at Casablanca in
January 1943. The night-time raids of Bomber Command were
agreed to be complementary to daylight raids of the 8th US Army
Air Force against selected military targets such as submarine
yards, oil installations and aircraft assembly plants. The agreed
policy was confirmed in a joint declaration that made no
reference either to terror bombing or to "generalised area attack"
as it was usually described in euphemistic British terms.[4] So it is
reasonable to deduce that the destruction of an entire city such as
Hamburg, although practically of no military advantage, probably
served a covert political purpose: the preparation of public
opinion for the ultimate nuclear firestorms that would soon
befall Hiroshima and Nagasaki.

The sustained attack on Hamburg, to impart a sense of
biblical mission, had appropriately been codenamed Gomorrah.
Its final death toll on the ground exceeded 45,000 — more than
the total number of Britons killed in the entire nine-months
"blitz" two years earlier. Nor was the carnage of Operation
Gomorrah and subsequent raids confined only to German
civilians. RAF Bomber Command, in relation to its size, started
suffering a greater casualty rate than any other branch of the
British armed forces.

In concerted attacks on Berlin, which commenced two
months after Operation Gomorrah and did not end until 16
major bombing operations were completed on 24 March the
following year, 492 Bomber Command aircraft failed to return.

Another 9 541 aircraft were damaged, of which 95 had to be written off as total wrecks — bringing the total loss to 587 bombers.[5] On the night of 30 March 1944, in an attack on Nuremberg, Bomber Command suffered its heaviest casualties in a single raid of the entire war: 545 airmen killed with negligible damage to the German war effort.[6] One British rear-gunner witnessed the night skies above Germany being lit up by the flashes of "bombers blowing up at the rate of about one a minute".[7] Harris, in his memoirs, would not even bother to mention this particular raid.

The self-assuredness with which Harris ignored the officially stated policy of selective, precision attacks on specified military targets, and the conspicuous absence of official reprimand in this regard, could only mean he had some kind of "sanction" higher than that of the Chief of Air Staff or the Air Ministry. Only Churchill could have provided such "sanction" — the legitimacy of which nonetheless remains open to conjecture. The RAF's official Director of Bomber Operations, Air Commodore Sidney Bufton, was not even consulted on major terror bombing operations such as the raid on Hamburg, news of its destruction coming to him after the event "like a bolt from the blue".[8]

Of many attacks carried out by Bomber Command in 1943, only an exceptional attack on Kassel, on 25 October, complied with official targeting policy. The Kassel attack, although taking the lives of 5,200 German civilians, helped delay Germany's V-2 flying-bomb production programme — proving that Bomber Command, when instructed by Harris to do so, was quite capable of attacking important military targets with impressive results.[9] This was otherwise in marked contrast to his contemptuous disregard for official targeting policy specifying attacks on enemy fighter aircraft production plants. As a consequence of Harris's omissions, German fighter aircraft production was allowed to soar, with the result that large numbers of *Luftwaffe* fighters started decimating the American day-time strategic bomber formations. In just one attack against military targets in Germany on 14 October the Americans lost 60 of their Flying Fortresses out of 291.[10]

Government information policy in the meantime was consistently to deny that German civilians were being systematically slaughtered, but nothing was done to discourage some newspapers from urging Bomber Command, as the Sunday Express did on 5 September 1943, to "Coventrate 42 Reich towns". By 21 October the London Daily Telegraph was congratulating Harris: "Hamburg has had the equivalent of at least 60 'Coventrys', Cologne 17, Dusseldorf 12 and Essen 10." Some suggestions in Britain that the nation was losing moral superiority to the Germans were fobbed off with official public assurances to the effect that the government was adhering fully to the principle of attacking only military targets. In private, however, the Air Minister Sir Archibald Sinclair admitted to Chief of Air Staff, Sir Charles Portal, that the government did not wish to "provoke the leaders of religious and humanitarian opinion to protest".[11]

Portal, with the concurrence of the Chiefs of Staff — Britain's official war strategists — had long since abandoned his support for "generalised aerial bombardment". Both Portal and the Chiefs of Staff were now in an embarrassing situation: Bomber Command was essentially a Command out of control — a lost Command. While Bomber Command's operations retained every appearance of being the responsibility of Portal and the Chief's of Staff, it was in fact under the illegitimate and non-attributable control of Churchill and his junta-like circle. Until the end of the war it would remain a crucial issue for the Air Ministry to re-establish control over Bomber Command without anyone having sufficient authority or the boldness to challenge Harris's links with Churchill, and Churchill's omniscient behind-the-scenes caucus.[12] It would have taken real discipline not to perceive what all of it meant. Fortunately, the military-political elite were well-disciplined, so it all passed in silence. But as 1943 drew to a close, Labour MP Richard Stokes asked the Air Minister in Parliament whether the official policy of limiting the objectives of Bomber Command to targets of military importance had changed to the bombing of civilians. Sir Archibald replied: "The honourable gentleman is incorrigible. I have indicated a series of vitally important military objectives."[13] Needless to say, the steady destruction of German urban centres continued unabated, with Harris remaining true to his ambition of "maintaining a destruction rate of two and a half cities per month".[14] At the same time, Air Ministry publications promoted an official aura of mystique around the operations of Bomber Command, describing them as "somewhat of an experimental nature". One may plausibly conjecture that the "experimental nature" of such operations was aimed at conditioning of a core public attitude of consent that would pave the way for using against civilians an ultimate terror weapon — the atomic bomb, then nearing completion at Los Alamos.

Even or especially in the belated build-up to the Allied invasion of Normandy, and with the Red Army still engaging four-fifths of Hitler's forces on the eastern front, Harris remained unremitting in his refusal to attack military targets. Instead of destroying gun emplacements, beach defences, communications systems or ammunition dumps in occupied France, he ordered the bombers to destroy no fewer than twelve German towns and cities, most of which made an insignificant contribution to the overall German war effort.[15] When the Normandy landings eventually began on June 6, 1944, and when he was supposed to be acting in support of the invading Western armies, Harris remained fully committed to indiscriminate terror bombing. He also continued purposefully to abstain from any operation that might shorten the war or be of any assistance to the Russians. This was particularly so in relation to German aircraft factories producing fighter aircraft. Apart from the fact that *Luftwaffe* fighters were still decimating the American daylight strategic bombing formations, the outcome of the critical operations on the Russian front depended very largely on the enemy's ability to maintain in operation a certain strength of fighter aircraft. For this reason the German fighter aircraft factories had been identified by the Air Ministry for specific targeting.[16] Yet while Harris ignored official policy with impunity, help for the Russians on the eastern Front continued concurrently to loom large in Churchill's public justifications for bombing operations as a proxy second front. On this pretext, after a personal meeting with Stalin, he had boosted the RAF's manpower allocation for 1943 by one third above what had been requested by the Secretary of State for Air.[17]

Harris, in addition to his open disregard for Air Ministry directives advising him to attack German fighter aircraft factories, similarly held himself aloof from attacking German oil installations, which had been unanimously identified by the Combined Chiefs of Staff as a war-winning strategic target. A potential German oil shortage had long been noted by the Combined Chiefs of Staff, and they had repeatedly but without success urged immediate, attacks upon the Ploesti oil fields of Nazi-occupied Rumania, Germany's main source of supply. From August 1944 onwards it had been Portal's view that bombing attacks should be concentrated on Germany's essential war supplies, especially oil supplies. The Chiefs of Staff had concurred, and Portal's view was explicitly conveyed to Churchill.[18] Churchill simply ignored Portal's recommendations in favour of his own style of war management. When Harris did grudgingly bring himself to launch a few attacks on this potentially war-winning target, the raids were desultory and half-hearted. German Armaments Minister Albert Speer was pleased to observe that "the Allies threw away success when it was already in their hands".[19] Only when the Red Army finally captured the largely intact Ploesti oil fields did the *Luftwaffe* eventually start running out of fuel. There were also synthetic oil plants scattered throughout eastern Germany, which similarly benefited from Harris's aversion for selective precision attack — an aberration to which Stalin had already drawn Churchill's attention.[20] The fiction was maintained throughout this period that "strategic" bombing was a legitimate means of conducting hostilities "in support of Russia", while the bombing campaign was promoted publicly as the most effective way to halt Germany in its tracks. This despite the fact that essential war production was visibly surviving in Germany at a time when its destruction was supposed to be the critical measuring rod of bombing policy.

All Allied attempts to make "strategic" bombing a weapon of some precision to be systematically applied against German war production were never properly implemented by Harris, yet Bomber Command continued to receive the lion's share of resources on the pretext of aiding Russia. These two factors, heavy political rhetoric favouring aerial bombardment as a proxy second front to relieve pressure on the Russians, coupled with the proven chronic ineffectiveness of the bombing effort, go a long way towards revealing the true nature of Churchill's rationale. Bringing the war to a rapid end while the Russians were sustaining heavy losses was not among his strategic priorities.

By the end of 1944, Harris was a source of great inconvenience to the Air Ministry and to Portal in particular. Faced with mounting criticism to the effect that war-winning opportunities were being spurned, Portal expressed his "profound disappointment" to Harris. "If I knew you to be so wholehearted in the attack on oil as in the past you have in the matter of attacking cities," Portal complained bitterly, "I would have little to worry about."[21] Compounding Portal's frustration was the fact that the media had, over a period of years, been encouraged to erect around Harris the popular image of a national hero. Portal knew it would be difficult to get rid of

Harris or reverse the weight of public opinion behind him. This mass of opinion, in turn, was largely a consequence of the Air Ministry's own propaganda campaigns; and it would have been extremely difficult to now get the media to re-examine the very same false assumptions it had helped propagate in the first place. Portal was thus in an impossible situation partly of his own making.

The war in the air was by this time being conducted very much on the Western Allies' own terms, the ratio of combat aircraft alone standing at five to one in their favour.[22] Yet, even with victory nearly in their grasp, Harris persisted with the terror bombing campaign when he was supposed to be acting in support of the Allied armies during the invasion of Normandy. Friend and foe alike fell prey to his bombs. Four hundred British casualties resulted on 14 August, when Bomber Command succeeded in bombing some of the British Army's own positions in France.[23] At Caen, in the same month, 6,000 heavy bombs were dropped into a residential area less than three miles square — although there was no sign of enemy tanks or gun emplacement.[24] French anger increased as the port of Le Havre was attack by Harris's bombers on 2 September in an operation that had no clear military purpose, German defences were untouched and the German garrison did not surrender for another week. Between two and three thousand French civilians were killed — many of them members of the underground resistance. Local inhabitants were appalled at the senseless destruction caused by their "British" liberators. The communist-led resistance movement protested strongly against a bombing raid on Marseilles in particular, pointing out that, given the necessary support and explosives they themselves would have done the job far more effectively and at no cost in civilian lives.[25]

In Eastern Europe, meanwhile, not only had the Red Army survived the most critical phase in the greatest battle in history, it was actually on the point of heading for Berlin. Red

Army commander Marshal Georgi Zhukov, having liberated Poland and Czechoslovakia and now poised to advance his troops through eastern Germany, noted he was being provided by Western intelligence with information that "failed to conform with reality". Emanating from "certain sources" in the West, Zhukov suspected this was intended "to confuse both the Anglo-American and the Soviet commands and divert the Soviet Command's attention away from the area the Germans are preparing for the main offensive operation on the eastern front". Churchill in particular was singled out by Zhukov, who suspected him of nurturing secret plans for the entire post-war reorganisation of the central European states headed by pro-Western governments.[26] It was not a benign proposition.

Earlier, the *London News Chronicle* with a circulation of 1.2 million readers, had published a 1943 Gallup poll in which Britons and Americans placed their respective countries embarrassingly low on a list of those nations contributing to the war effort. There was by contrast great public admiration for the Red Army's counter-offensive and its continuing achievements on the eastern front. Churchill lamented in private: "This is one of the worst things that has happened in the newspaper world since the war began."[27] The worst was yet to come. The entire front page of Britain's popular *Sunday Pictorial* was taken up on 24 October 1943 by a vivid account of the Red Army's breaching of the Dnieper, again unassisted by its Western "allies". Under a bold headline proclaiming "The Greatest Battle Ever Known", the paper recalled that "the Russians have been fobbed off with promises of a Second Front for eighteen long and tantalising months. Either the Government was fooling itself or it was attempting to fool somebody else — and not only someone in Berlin." Reflecting a widely held opinion in Britain at that time, the *Pictorial* continued:

True, the Russians may not care any more. They are well

on the way to winning this war on their own, and they may regard all our threats and promises with sublime indifference. Nobody will blame them if they do, but it is absolutely imperative that our future relations with what is now proved to be the greatest military power in Europe should not be compromised by people who have promised so glibly and fulfilled not at all.

Previous British governments had preached that communism was a vastly inferior social, economic and political system. But according to a confidential Home Office intelligence report there was now an "almost unanimous" belief that the successes of the Red Army were due in large part to the superior efficiency of communism. Membership of the British Communist Party, in the course of just 18 months, had increased more than fourfold from 12,000 in June 1941 to a staggering 56,000 by the end of 1942.[28] Which was why in the following year the Ministry of Information came up with the idea of "stealing the thunder" from the Left. The ministry, striving to prevent the British Communist Party from taking further initiative, instructed its regional information officers to arrange Anglo-Soviet friendship campaigns "before the communists had a chance to do so". A vast celebration was organised at the Albert Hall to commemorate Red Army Day, the twenty-fifth anniversary of the founding of the Red Army.[29]

In the fullness of time, the Soviet Union would be less accommodating. Churchill would be swift to object when Stalin demanded that terror bombing be included in the list of war crimes judged at Nuremberg.

As for Bomber Commands own casualties, a number of observers have compared the slaughter of Bomber Command pilots and aircrew with the carnage wreaked on infantry battalions in the trenches of World War 1. Harris, paradoxically, was attracted to the idea of "strategic" bombing because he wanted to avoid a repetition of senseless casualties on the ground. He had written of his ostensible revulsion at the memory of "morons volunteering to get hung in the wire and shot in the stomach in the mud of Flanders."[30]

The affair of the Lost Command and the special relationship that existed behind the scenes between Churchill and Harris have never been officially explained. But whatever else he might have been, Harris was clearly no intellectual giant. He would have been easy prey for someone of Churchill's calibre.

Part Two

COLD WAR: 1944 — 1990

Chapter 6:

War in the Shadows

On January 1, 1947, the British and American forces in post-war Germany merged their respective zones of occupation into a single unified zone called Bizonia, handing over much of the administrative responsibility for running Bizonia to the West Germans under British and American supervision. Plans were made at the same time for the economic merger of the French zone with Bizonia to produce a federated West Germany. All this was bitterly opposed by the Soviet Union. It rightly saw in these developments the establishment of a separatist German government in occupied Germany, and a blatant contravention of earlier agreements reached at the historic Yalta conference between Britain, America and the Soviet Union shortly before the war ended. It had been agreed in particular that a defeated Germany would be ruled by a four-power Allied Control Council including the Soviet Union. But now Britain and America had entered into a separate agreement between themselves, and the Allied Control Council had in effect ceased to exist as an organ of government.

In mid-June 1948 the Soviet Union was finally goaded into massive retaliation when the West substituted the *Reichsmark* with a brand new currency printed in America, the *Deutsche Mark*, as the official currency in West Germany. The Soviet Union immediately stopped all passenger traffic between the Western zones and Berlin by road and rail. On the autobahn at the Helmstedt checkpoint, Russian guards turned back all eastbound traffic. At the border station of Marienborn trains carrying German passengers and military goods were also turned back. Patrols of Russian and East German frontier guards were greatly increased in strength along the entire length of the Soviet zonal border. The Russians also imposed major electricity cuts. More than two million inhabitants of the British, French and American zones of Berlin were cut off from contact with the West. The blockade of Berlin had begun.*

Many historians and other ideological managers of Western society — teachers, journalists and the like — would in future years attribute the commencement of the political Cold War between East and West to the Berlin blockade of 1947. They are all wrong, though the myth survives to this day. The fact is, the origins of the Cold War are firmly embedded in World War II, when Churchill and his elite cabal secretly waged a shadow war against communism under the guise of fighting the Nazis and "helping" the Soviet Union. This much is clear from Churchill's protracted reticence in opening a second front in Europe. Even when the Western Allies did eventually launch their belated invasion of the continent, the shadow war against the Soviet Union continued unabated. If anything, it might even have been stepped up.

With the invasion of Normandy on D-Day on June 6, 1944 the terms of warfare in occupied France had ceased to be ostensibly those of Hitler and became obviously those of the

---

* Britain, America and their allies then decided to vault over the Russian blockade and supply Berlin by air. On June 26, 1948, the commander of the US Air Forces in Europe ordered an air-lift to begin. Hundreds of transport aircraft from the West brought more than half a million tons of food to Berlin in the course of more than 550,000 sorties over the next 13 months. On May 12, 1949, the Soviet Union lifted the Berlin blockade, which had clearly failed. Eleven days later, the Federal Republic of Germany was created out of the Western zones. (See Douglas Botting, *From the Ruins of the Reich: Germany 1945-1949*, New York: New American Library, 1985).

Allied Expeditionary Force. No amount of posturing, prevarication and empty promises on the part of Churchill could hide this fact. The cross-channel build-up provided the Expeditionary Force with at least twice the number of men, four times the number of tanks, and six times the number of aircraft available to the enemy. On D-day itself the Germans had mustered only 319 aircraft against 12,837 of the Western Allies whose military strength soon increased to the point where they had effective superiority of 20 to one in tanks and 25 to one in aircraft.

Yet, despite its vast numerical superiority and other advantages in its favour, the offensive of the Allied Expeditionary Force was characterised by restraint. Compared with the Russians, who still bore the brunt of fighting on the eastern front, the invading force was merely playing about. It had 91 full-strength divisions facing Germany's 60 weak divisions whose overall strength was roughly equal to only 26 complete divisions. The invasion force, consisting of British, American and Canadian troops, thus engaged less than a third of the total number of German divisions in France, while the Red Army engaged 185 enemy divisions in the east. For every German division engaged by the Western armies, the Red Army met three. In terms of armoured units alone, of the roughly 5,000 tanks available to Germany, more than 4,000 were deployed on the eastern front. [1] So obvious was the disparity, most of the German divisions having been deployed to fight Russia on the eastern front, that in real terms a western front hardly even existed.

The invading force's lethargic ground offensive was characterised by such obvious restraint as to cause bitter resentment within some of the top-most British military echelons. In the words of Major General John Kennedy, then Assistant Chief of the General Staff: "For six weeks or so, (after the invasion) the Germans did not attempt or even desire to move their divisions in the Pas de Calais or elsewhere towards the scene of action in Normandy."[2] The West's failure to launch a concerted ground attack on the enemy was similarly noted by the British Vice-Chief of General Staff, General Sir David Fraser:

> For a little while — a few weeks of August and September (1944) — the Western Front was open, and a determined effort on our part might have finished the war, with incalculable strategic and political consequences, and with a saving of the huge number of casualties suffered later ... it was the last chance to seize this great strategic opportunity. It failed, and the war went on."[3]

In Holland, General Montgomery's stated objective in September 1944 was for British and American tanks and paratroopers to capture bridges across various canals and rivers. But crucial intelligence derived from Ultra intercepts and decrypts, and from agents providing detailed reports of enemy movements and reinforcements in the area, was either ignored or did not reach Montgomery. On September 17 two American and one British airborne divisions were dropped as an "airborne carpet" between Eindhoven and Arnhem. A ground link-up was to have been affected with Montgomery's 21st Army Group within two to three days. The agreed plan was that once the lower Rhine was crossed, operations would then be expanded against the Ruhr to bring an early end to the war. Over 7,000 men, more than two thirds of the 1st Airborne Division, were dropped in the Arnhem area, where British intelligence had indicated only a maximum opposition of brigade strength.

The enemy's reaction was one of astonishment at their good fortune. Arnhem and its environs had been chosen by the Germans as a suitable place in which to refit two entire divisions of the 2nd SS Panzer Corps, which were available immediately to contest the landings. Their reaction was swift and without mercy:

At the key Arnhem bridge, 1,200 British paratroopers — the cream of the British Army — were killed and more than 3,000 taken prisoner. That was only the start of an overall debacle in Holland, resulting in a total Allied loss exceeding 17,000 killed, wounded and missing in action.[4]

Scarce air transport resources had been diverted from useful operations elsewhere to the disastrous paratroop drop at Arnhem. The Commander in Chief of 2nd Tactical Air Force, Air Marshal Arthur Coningham complained bitterly that "the freezing of air transport during a week of fine weather, with ample ground suitable for landings, when the American and British armies were only halted through lack of fuel and ammunition supply, was the decisive factor in preventing our armies reaching the Rhine before the onset of winter".[5] A further eight months would pass before Arnhem was finally captured — just a month before the war in Europe ended. Montgomery, soon to be promoted to Field-Marshal and for the sake of immediate press reaction, described the disaster at Arnhem as "a 90 percent success" — drawing from Prince Bernhard of the Netherlands the bitter retort: "My country can never again afford the luxury of a Montgomery success."[6]

There were similar "successes" occurring elsewhere along the western front. In Belgium, where the stated intention of Supreme Headquarters Allied Expeditionary Force (SHAEF) was to capture the crucial maritime port of Antwerp, SHAEF disregarded explicit intelligence warnings that the Germans were about to secure the approaches to the port. The invading force, failing to move swiftly on the offensive before the Germans completed defence preparations, ended up with Antwerp rendered entirely useless to them for the next six months. This made it impossible for an immediate advance on the Ruhr or on Berlin, which would have been practicable only if Montgomery's 40 divisions could be supplied through Antwerp.[7]

Virtually the same kind of deliberate stalling,

procrastination and prolongation of the war had occurred months earlier at Anzio in Italy, where the Germans were wholly unprepared for amphibious landings. Excellent conditions had existed here for providing substantial relief to the Red Army on the eastern front by launching a determined Allied thrust northwards through Italy. SHAEF clearly ignored available intelligence showing conditions to be ideal for an immediate and unopposed advance on Rome. Instead, the military command waited until the Germans had organised an effective defence and counter-attack. The New Zealand and Indian contingents of the landing force took particularly heavy casualties, with the enemy then retiring north of Rome in good order. There the Germans established a new and unyielding line in Tuscany where the Italian campaign would drag on for at least another year, at a cost of many more courageous Allied lives sacrificed on the altar of deception.[8]

A final debacle in the patterned distribution of epic intelligence "failures" and unheroic command decisions occurred in December 1944, when the invading force failed to anticipate the German offensive in the Ardennes — the Battle of the Bulge, where the Germans inflicted major casualties on the Anglo-American armies and nearly halted the Allied advance in its tracks. Field Marshal Albrecht Kesselring was later to reveal that Germany's 10th Army, the defending force in Italy, was so unprepared that it would have been virtually annihilated had the Western Allies immediately advanced their attack once a beach-head was established.[9]

With the command structure of the Allied Expeditionary Force thus masquerading as "liberators" while actually prolonging the war, Churchill was busily engaged behind the scenes in intervening persistently in the Anglo-American nuclear weapons project. He continually spurred the Los Alamos scientists to more vigorous efforts in producing an atomic bomb before the Russians single-handedly won the war in Europe. Churchill could count on the unwavering support of Roosevelt who was fully prepared, hopeful even, to use the atomic bomb against Germany.[10] The Red Army's momentous breakthrough into eastern Germany, and its inexorable advance on Berlin, then in progress, threatened to turn into reality not only the worst fears of Hitler but also those of the Western leadership. Britain's Foreign Secretary Anthony Eden had in 1941 already warned that Russian prestige at the end of the war would be so great that "the establishment of communist governments in the majority of European countries would be greatly facilitated".[11] Similar fears had also been conveyed to Churchill by his South African ally, General Jan Smuts, who complained in 1943:

> I have the uncomfortable feeling that the scale and speed of our land operations leaves much to be desired ... Almost all the honours on land go to the Russians, and deservedly so, considering the scale and speed of their fighting and the magnificence of their strategy on a vast front. Surely our performance can be bettered and the comparison with Russia rendered less unflattering to us? To the ordinary man it must appear that it is Russia who is winning the war. If this impression continues, what will be our post-war world position compared with that of Russia? A tremendous shift in our world status may follow, and leave Russia the diplomatic master of the world. This is both unnecessary and undesirable, and would have especially bad reactions for the British Commonwealth.[12]

Similar fears had been expressed to Roosevelt in Washington by his Chiefs of Staff who warned the American president in August 1944: "The end of the war will produce a change in the pattern of military strength more comparable ... with that occasioned by the fall of Rome than with any other change during the succeeding fifteen hundred years."[13]

Neither Smuts nor the American Chiefs of Staff would have been aware, as Churchill and Roosevelt were, of the secret nuclear weapons project then nearing completion, and which would guarantee for them the achievement of post-war political goals in Europe. The atomic bomb, however, had not yet been tested, and with few urban dwellings left to set on fire in western Germany, Churchill and the bomber barons needed another means by which to demonstrate at close quarters to the Russians an uncontested margin of military if not moral superiority over them.

The fate of Dresden was sealed. Although the city was only of very minor importance to the overall German war effort, it lay conveniently across the Red Army's direct line of advance to Berlin. Famous for its china and architecture, Dresden was also the largest of very few civilian areas remaining intact in the whole of Germany.[14] It also happened to be crowded with large numbers of civilian refugees who had fled from bombing in other parts of Germany, its population of 600,000 having more than doubled to 1,250,000. Since January 26, 1945 special trains had delivered thousands of evacuees to the city, most recently on the afternoon of February 12, while thousands more arrived on foot or in horse-drawn carts.[15] What followed was to be one of the most senseless acts of savagery ever known to humankind.

In the early hours of February 14, Ash Wednesday, a total of 778 RAF heavy bombers began the attack. The following day the Americans attacked with almost as many aircraft again. They somehow managed to overlook the fact that 26,000 Allied prisoners of war were imprisoned in the suburbs of Dresden. When the last of the bombers departed, the open spaces on the banks of the Elbe were piled with the bodies of civilians who flocked to the river in search of escape from the heat and then drowned. The bodies of many others were glued to the surface of streets where the tarmac had melted and then solidified as the firestorm engulfed 11 square miles — an area much larger than that destroyed at Hamburg. About 75 percent of all property was gutted completely as temperatures soared to around 1,000 degrees Centigrade.[16] Apart from the many victims it incinerated immediately, thousands more died in air raid shelters as the firestorm sucked out oxygen which was replaced with poisonous fumes. About 50,000 civilians were killed — around 10,000 more than those who perished in the Hamburg firestorm, and 20,000 more than those killed during the entire eight-months "blitz" on Britain. Countless numbers of people were rendered homeless. Bomber Command casualties were negligible — Germany's earlier loss of France to the Allied Expeditionary Force had created a gaping hole in Hitler's early-warning radar system, providing the RAF with unchallenged operational omnipotence.[17]

Astonishingly, almost unbelievably, Dresden was attacked again on March 2, this time by the Americans alone. Mustang fighter escorts machine-gunned fleeing civilians while the heavy B-17s achieved the singular distinction of sinking a hospital ship on the Elbe, filled with injured from the earlier raids.[18]

Dresden did not contain any oil refineries or synthetic oil plants, unlike Brux to the south, or Bohlen, Ruhland and Politz which remained untouched, to the north and west of the doomed city. Nor did Dresden appear on any list of priority targets issued weekly by the Combined Strategic Targets Committee. Any military justification for the American and the British raids was non-existent, damage in terms of "war production" being confined solely to the German cigar and cigarette industry.[19] Nor did the destruction of Dresden disrupt or delay the Red Army's continued, rapid advance on Berlin from the east. This probably came as something of a disappointment to Harris who had issued briefing notes to Bomber Command aircrews stating modestly that an "incidental" purpose of the massed aerial attack on Dresden was to show the Russians, then just a few miles from Dresden, "what Bomber Command can do".[20] The inference to be drawn from this is that Harris, at the behest of Churchill, wished to convey to the Russians a vivid impression of the

West's overwhelming superiority in long-distance aerial bombardment and the ability of British and American aircraft to demolish an entire city in the space of just a few hours. Indeed, the demolition of Dresden may be interpreted as an act of outright intimidation stopping just short of direct military operations against the USSR.

Marshal Zhukov had given the order for the Red Army's main assault on German front lines on June 22, 1944 — the third anniversary of Hitler's invasion of the Soviet Union — when 26,000 heavy guns and rocket launchers, 4,000 tanks and 1.6 million Soviet soldiers started advancing along a front of more than 500 miles. Soon the Red Army, including full divisions of Poles and Czechs, had reached the gates of Warsaw . It had also captured the high passes of the Carpathians, which command the entrances to Slovakia and Hungary. Along the Baltic coast the German army had been encircled and would soon be annihilated. The road to Berlin had been opened.

Against this background, the destruction of Dresden was recommended by Churchill "with the particular object of exploiting the confused conditions which are likely to exist ... during the successful Russian advance".[21] Before the massacre, No.1 Group, Bomber Command, had been told during pre-flight briefing that Dresden was to be bombed because it was "a railway centre"; No.3 Group was duped into believing it would be attacking "a German army headquarters"; No.6 Group was misinformed that Dresden was "an important industrial area, producing chemicals and munitions"; some squadrons were deceptively assured that Dresden contained a Gestapo headquarters and a large poison-gas plant; another Group was given the impression that the bombers would be breaching the defences of a "fortress city" essential to the Germans in their fight against the advancing Russians.[22]

Whatever impression the Russians themselves might have gained from taking possession of a ruined city after having witnessed at close quarters the destructive potential of the West's long-distance bombers, this was probably not what the Red Army had in mind when on February 4, 10 days before the Dresden atrocity, it had conveyed to the Western Allies an urgent request. The Red Army's Deputy Chief of Staff, Marshal Antonov had specifically asked the Western Allies as a matter of urgent priority to cripple the transportation system in eastern Germany. The request was reiterated by Marshal Khudyakov, Chief of the Soviet Air Staff. Both commanders urgently wished to prevent enemy troop movements toward the eastern front, particular reference being made by Khudyakov to the necessity of preventing the movement by road and rail of German reinforcements from Italy.[23]

The request was ignored. Dresden's crowded Dresden-Klotzche airfield remained unscathed, and the railway marshalling yards were similarly spared destruction.[24] Yet highly advanced and extremely accurate ground-attack fighter-bombers and dive-bombers of the Anglo-American 2nd Tactical Air Force, then dispersed at various airfields in newly liberated Belgium, Holland and France, were readily available for such a task. Armed with rockets, light bombs and heavy machine guns, they had the easy capability to destroy German road and rail communications and generally harass the German armed forces deep in eastern Germany, without indiscriminately slaughtering civilians. So under-utilised was 2nd Tactical Air Force during these closing stages of the war that many of its aircraft were left neatly parked next to unprotected runways in Allied occupied territory where they were systematically destroyed on the ground by remnants of the Luftwaffe. In just one such raid, 200 brand-new fighter-bombers of the 2nd Tactical Air Force were destroyed at an airfield in Belgium, without any loss to the enemy.

The highly-decorated 2nd Tactical Air Force commander, Air Chief-Marshal Sir Trafford Leigh-Mallory, was at the centre of a bitter row with Britain's war planners over the merits of combined tactical operations in support of Allied ground forces, and "strategic" bombing conducted independently of combined operations.[25] The argument came to an abrupt end shortly after the destruction of Dresden, when Sir Trafford was suddenly transferred to the Far East. He was mysteriously killed when the aircraft that was transporting him to India crashed in the French Alps. The exact cause of the crash was never officially established.

As for events in eastern Germany immediately after the Dresden attacks, a blinding deference for the official version ensured that the British Broadcasting Corporation reported on 14 February that RAF and American bombers had "raided places of utmost importance to the Germans in their struggle against the Russians, notably at Dresden".[26] One press officer at Supreme HQ Allied Expeditionary Force was rather more forthcoming. In an "off the record" comment to war correspondents, a certain Air Commodore Grierson confirmed for the first time that the Allied plan in eastern Germany was to "bomb large population centres and then to prevent relief supplies from reaching and refugees from leaving them". Associated Press swiftly cabled this news to the world at large. The British censors reacted promptly, imposing a general clampdown on the report.[27]

A massacre of such magnitude as occurred at Dresden, however, was difficult to hide indefinitely. During a debate in the House of Commons on 6 March, the irrepressible Labour MP for Ipswich, Richard Stokes, quoted the Associated Press report and a German account which had appeared in the previous day's *Manchester Guardian*. For the first time the expression "terror bombing" was used in Parliament when Stokes complained:

> "... you will find people in the Army and Air Force protesting against this mass and indiscriminate slaughter from the air ... Leaving aside strategic bombing, which I question very much, and tactical bombing, with which I

agree if it is done with a reasonable degree of accuracy, there is no case whatever under any conditions in my view, for terror bombing".[28]

Air Minister Sir Archibald Sinclair left it to his deputy to reply to the debate. The relatively obscure Under-Secretary assured the House:

> We are not wasting bombers or time purely on terror tactics. It does not do the Honourable Member justice to ... suggest that there are a lot of Air Marshals or pilots ... sitting in a room thinking how many German women and children they can kill.[29]

Barely a week later on March 11, more than 1,000 of Harris's bombers carried out a heavy daylight raid on Essen, unleashing 4,700 tonnes of bombs which destroyed the city almost completely. On 12 March, Dortmund became the target of the heaviest of all raids in Europe so far when 1,107 bombers dropped 4,851 tonnes of bombs on the already almost completely destroyed city.[30] German war production in the period between January and the time of Germany's capitulation in May was reduced by a mere 1.2 percent.[31] British Intelligence analysts would have been well aware of this anomaly, given that Ultra had since 1944 been providing them with a great deal of reliable information about the German economy.[32]

While these final atrocities were taking place under the twin banners of "halting German war production" and "helping the Russians", Churchill took great pains to obscure the fact that the true fulcrum of air power lay neither with the Directorate of Bombing Operations, nor with the Air Ministry or the Chiefs of Staff, but solely with himself, Harris and a small cabal of handpicked confidants. Official documents suppressed for many years in the British archives but now available to researchers, contain a reproachful minute dated March 28 from Churchill to the Chiefs of Staff in which he deftly shifted all blame for the terror bombing onto the hapless Chiefs of Staff. It was they, according to Churchill, who had been principally responsible for "increasing the terror, though under other pretexts".[33] In a worried "most private and confidential" message to Harris, Churchill warned him to be "very careful ... not to admit that we ever did anything not justified by the circumstances and the actions of the enemy in the measures we took to bomb Germany."[34]

Meanwhile, undeterred by the measures of Churchill and Harris, the Red Army continued advancing inexorably on Berlin's heavily defended Reichstag, the symbolic heart of Nazidom. A few months earlier, in January 1945, the Red Army and the Western Allied armies were still approximately the same distance away from Berlin, even though the disparity of enemy forces facing them was heavily in favour of the Anglo-Americans. But by mid-April it was the Red Army that arrived first in Berlin and began engaging its defending troops in close combat.

Street by street, building by building, and finally staircase by staircase and cellar by cellar, Soviet soldiers inched their way forward through the city, taking heavy casualties in the fierce fighting. Finally, on 30 April a red flag bearing the hammer and sickle fluttered over the Reichstag. Three days later Berlin fell. After more than 1,000 days and nights of war along a front thousands of miles in length, as well as behind enemy lines in the occupied territories, a victorious Red Army marched through the Brandenburg Gate.[35]

The price paid by the Russians for defeating Hitler on the principal and decisive front of the war was enormous. Every minute of the war the Russians lost nine lives, 587 lives every hour and 14,000 lives every day, with two out of every five persons killed during the war being Soviet citizens. Hundreds of Russian towns and cities were devastated. Well over 20 million Russians, half of them civilians, had died — many more than the combined total military casualties of Germany and the Western Allies together.[36]

Chapter 7:

Atomic Blackmail

While news of the atomic explosions on 6 and 9 August might have come as a nasty shock to the world at large, the wiping out of entire cities did not. Earlier events at Harmburg and Dresden had seen to that. Besides which, on August 2, hundreds of US Strategic Air Force long-range bombers based in the Pacific had set a new record for the heaviest bombing raid of World War II, when they showered 6,000 tonnes of phosphorus bombs on four Japanese cities including Kawasaki. That particular raid, in turn, had been the culmination of a long series of similar raids in the months preceding the nuclear holocaust, when American air attacks on Japanese cities had mounted in frequency and intensity, leaving. more than 15 million Japanese civilians homeless. Nearly nine million of them had either fled or were preparing to flee into the countryside, leaving behind the corpses of more than a quarter million civilian dead. In one attack on the night of 9 March, 180,000 civilians died in Tokyo — described triumphantly by *Time* magazine as "a dream come true". About 40 percent of Japan's urban area was by then either destroyed or seriously damaged. Two million houses lay reduced to ashes in 66 different towns and cities, equal to 250 square miles of urban area.[1]

When news of atomic massacres in Japan reached the American public, early polls showed at least 80 percent of Americans approved of the atomic bombings while only one percent expressed any feeling of regret on the subject of more than 70,000 civilians killed instantly at Hiroshima and another 40,000 at Nagasaki. An NBC radio broadcast on August 6, which provided the first officially approved news of the first atomic explosion earlier that day, described Hiroshima as an important Japanese Army base. "The world will note," Truman announced personally, " that the first atomic bomb was dropped on Hiroshima, a military base. That was because we wished in this first attack to avoid, insofar as possible, the killing of civilians ... The Japanese began the war from the air at Pearl Harbour, they have been repaid manyfold."[2] He added that an invasion of Japan might have cost a million lives. US Secretary of State James Byrnes "corroborated" that the bombs had ended the war against Japan, and this had spared not only American lives but also those of "hundreds of thousands of American boys and millions more of Japanese people".[3]

The overwhelming response of the American media was one of euphoria. "Never was two billion dollars better spent," applauded *The Nation*, the bastion of American liberal opinion. *Readers Digest* added its voice to the ecstatic chorus, proclaiming that the nuclear massacres had shortened the war and saved American lives: "Never in all the long history of human slaughter have lives been lost to greater purpose", the *Digest* eulogised. *The Chicago Daily Tribune* on August 11 heaped similar praise on those who took the decision to drop the bombs. "Being merciless, they were merciful," the *Tribune* declared. Which was of course unmitigated nonsense.

If the American administration honestly believed the fabrications it was propagating, then it had clearly fallen prey to its own weapons of mass deception. Documents carefully preserved in Russian and German archives, and in the archives of the United States itself, would later disclose to researchers a very different set of circumstances surrounding the Western Allies' decision to mount nuclear attacks on Japan. Contrary to the Truman's claim, dutifully repeated by the media, that solely military considerations dictated use of the atomic bombs, the evidence points directly towards political considerations – in particular the ill-conceived consideration that atomic diplomacy would strengthen the West's hand against the USSR in determining post-war territorial gains.

A bizarre sequence of events had commenced immediately after the death of Roosvelt in April 1945, when there occurred a fundamental shift in US-Soviet relations. American power and the interpretation of the nation's requirements were placed in the hands of Harry S Truman and a small number of like-minded executive policy makers whose matching views of history and of the Soviet Union transformed US foreign policy. As a senator in July 1941, when the Nazi armies first launched their invasion of Russia, it was Truman who had unashamedly recommended: "If we see that Germany is winning the war we ought to help Russia, and if Russia is winning we ought to help Germany, and in that way let them kill as many as possible ..."[4]

Little had changed in Truman's demeanour four years later when he invited Soviet Foreign Minister Molotov to attend a meeting at the White House on April 23, 1945. As the Cold War historian DF Fleming describes it: "From the eminence of eleven days in power, Truman laid down the law to the Russians." For a start, Truman wanted the Red Army out of Poland, which the Russians had liberated from Nazi occupation without any help from the West. Nor did Truman appreciate the fact that Britain, France and America had effectively jettisoned Poland in 1939, thus contributing significantly to the conditions that precipitated World War II in the first place.[5]

Already Washington had begun reversing its earlier assurances to the USSR concerning economic assistance to help repair the tremendous material damage suffered by the USSR, which amounted to a staggering $485 billion at 1945 prices. Roosevelt had promised Stalin a multi-million dollar reconstruction loan without strings attached, but Truman now wanted the Russians to succumb instead to a newly devised Marshall Aid Plan. The plan imposed hegemonic conditions in terms of a European Recovery Programme, designed to revive European capitalism under United States influence. Dutifully supported by Britain as the other reserve currency country, America was set to write the economic rules in Europe to suit itself.[6]

There were significant reversals on the intelligence front as well. Even before the war with Germany was officially over, secret arrangements had been concluded between former key figures in the anti-communist section of German military intelligence and their American counterparts. Nazi spymaster Reinhard Gehlen was flown secretly to Washington by the American secret service, together with a bemedalled retinue consisting of one colonel, a lieutenant-colonel and two majors of the former Nazi General Staff. Accompanying them were their copious anti-communist intelligence files, preserved intact and containing information derived in part from the torture, interrogation and murder by starvation of about 4,000,000 prisoners. Gehlen and his retinue believed with considerable justification that Germany's future revival lay in Britain becoming as militarily efficient as possible in preparation for an ideological confrontation with Russia. In return for immunity from prosecution for war crimes, Gehlen promised to serve the West as faithfully as he had served Hitler. His offer was enthusiastically accepted, and Gehlen commenced immediately advising the Americans on how to go about establishing their own anti-Soviet networks in Europe.[7]

Rival US intelligence agencies of the occupation forces in Europe, meanwhile, were fighting like vultures for possession of captured Nazi anti-communist intelligence — giving rise to what the President of the Joint Intelligence Committee described in confidence as "violent quarrels between the American services whose representatives have used in my room most violent language about each other."[8] The round of aggressive politico-military jostling did not end there. The Western leadership was flexing its muscles to influence foreign policy decisions that would leave Germany divided into a series of military zones of occupation with Berlin as the seat of a proposed four-power control, well within the Soviet Zone of Occupation. By May 16, Stalin was warning his closest advisers that Churchill was preserving German forces in the British Zone of Occupation "in full combat readiness and co-operating with them" at a time when the Germans were supposed to be surrendering in hundreds of thousands.

This co-operation, according to the German historian Marius Steinert, was in preparation for a possible British military confrontation with Stalin and Tito — both of whom commanded great admiration among the British rank and file.[9] Already Churchill had instructed the head of the British Army, Field Marshal Viscount Alanbrooke, to investigate the possibility of fighting Russia before British and American forces were demobilised. The resultant study made it clear the best Churchill could hope for was to drive the Russians back to about the same line the Germans had reached earlier.[10]. So, Churchill envisioned a future role for the Germans in augmenting Montgomery's Anglo-American 21st Army Group in the event of hostilities with the USSR. Montgomery was instructed to be careful in stacking confiscated German arms so that they could be re-issued swiftly to the same men they had been confiscated from.[11]

Events in the Far East, however, placed restraints on any real or notional prospect of open hostilities breaking out between Britain and the Soviet Union-supported Yugoslavia. Despite the military setbacks Japan was experiencing at home, its well-developed war industry on the Asian continent remained intact. By relying on an industrial base in occupied Manchuria and Korea, the 700,000-strong Japanese Kwantung army of occupation in northern China could offer resistance for a long time to come. A major problem facing the Western powers in mid-1945 was how to eject this occupation force at a time when America's own land forces were still no nearer to the Japanese mainland than the two islands of Iwo Jima and Okinawa. Russian intervention in the war with Japan appeared to be the only solution. US Intelligence was of the opinion that Russia's entry into the war against Japan would "convince most Japanese at once of the inevitability of complete defeat".[12] Truman concurred, telling Associated Press that "more than anything else" the West needed the co-operation of the Soviet Union in order to step up the assault on Japan and its conquered territories, and such a move had already been agreed between Truman, Stalin and Churchill during their historical February 5 meeting at Yalta.[13]

But then, just as Churchill and Truman were preparing to meet Stalin at Potsdam in Germany on July 16, they received news of a successful, secret atomic bomb test in far-off New Mexico. Churchill was overjoyed. He knew the West no longer needed the Russians in any way. In his own words: "The end of the war no longer depended upon the pouring in of their armies ... We had no need to ask favours of them". In short, the atomic weapon and the power to use it altered completely the diplomatic equilibrium and redressed the Western position. "We were in the presence of a new factor in human affairs," Churchill enthused. "We possessed powers which were irresistible ... our outlook on the future was transformed".[14]

The potential consequences of Russian participation in the war against Japan would have had enormous geo-political implications. In return for intervention against Japan, Russia would have reacquired territories lost to Japan in 1904, namely the strategic Kurile Islands and the southern half of Sakhalien, as well as recovering a controlling position in the Manchurian region of China. This would have placed the USSR in a dominant position in continental north-east Asia. It would also have gained an assured stake in Japan's post-war affairs, and created a decisive shift in the world balance of power.[15] At the same time, linking up with Mao Tse Tung's guerilla forces who were in the process of driving out the Japanese occupiers, could serve as a catalyst in transforming all China into the world's largest communist state. In sum, there existed the strong potential for a new correlation of forces in the region, showing every sign of filling the vacuum brought about by the impending defeat of Japan and the eradication of British and French colonialism in Asia. This naturally failed to conform with America's own expansionist ambitions.

When Truman was presented with details of the A-bomb test, his position toward the Russians hardened noticeably. As sole possessor of the bomb, Truman had good reason to expect easier future dealings with Stalin. Even before the A-bomb was tested successfully, he confided to one of his closest advisers: "If it explodes, as I think it will, I'll certainly have a hammer on those boys (the Russians)".[16] The fate of Hiroshima and Nagasaki was accordingly decided with hardly a moment's discussion among the Western leaders. There was, in Churchill's words, "unanimous, automatic, unquestioned agreement (to use the bomb); nor did I ever hear the slightest suggestion that we should do otherwise."[17] Reflecting official thinking on the subject, US Secretary of State James Byrnes, was "most anxious to get the Japanese affair over with before the Russians get in. Once in the Far East, it would not be easy to get them out". Using the atomic bomb against Japanese cities in order to win the war was, in Byrnes' official view, a secondary matter. More important was that America's possession and demonstration of the bomb would "make the Russians more manageable".[18]

There is no question that ending the war against Japan before Russia entered it was a major, perhaps even the sole factor in the atomic decision. Stalin had earlier acceded to Western requests at the Yalta conference in February that the reinforced Red Army in the Far East would be poised to launch a two-pronged attack on the Japanese front in Manchuria on August 8.[19] An announcement of Soviet participation against Japan would certainly have tipped the balance and forced an immediate Japanese surrender without recourse to the nuclear massacres on August 6 and 9. Undeterred by the first nuclear explosion, and only hours before the second atomic bomb was dropped August 9, the Red Army launched its agreed attack against Japanese occupation forces in Manchuria. Historians are generally agreed that the Soviet Union's entry into the war against Japan was as effective as the two atomic blasts in causing the Japanese to surrender.

Apart from the more than 111,000 Japanese civilians who were killed immediately in the two explosions that ended the war and "saved millions of lives", the question of many subsequent deaths due to radioactive contamination was studiously avoided. Immediately after publication of the first report dispatched from Tokyo mentioning the radioactive contamination or "radiation sickness" that afflicted about 370,000 survivors of the two explosions. General Douglas MacArthur, in enforcing the withdrawal of all press correspondents from the city, had declared on September 5: "It is not military policy for correspondents to spearhead the occupation."[20] On September 19 the general headquarters of the occupation forces in Tokyo imposed censorship on all radio broadcasts and on newspapers, magazines and other print media. It prohibited reports, commentaries and treatises including those about radiation symptoms.[21]

Truman's claim that the decision to drop the atomic bombs was taken in order to "save lives" has been shown by historians to have no basis in official military planning documents. In fact, the very opposite is true. After the war, the official United States Strategic Bombing Survey would conclude:

"Hiroshima and Nagasaki were chosen as targets because of their concentration of population."[22] General Dwight Eisenhower, expressing "grave misgivings" over Truman's political decision to use the atomic bombs, notes in his memoirs:

> Japan was already defeated ... dropping the bomb was completely unnecessary (and) no longer mandatory as a measure to save American lives. It was my belief that Japan was, at that very moment, seeking some way to surrender with a minimum loss of face.[23]

Even Churchill, despite his enthusiastic participation in the decision to use the nuclear weapon, admits sheepishly in his memoirs that the defeat of Japan "was certain before the first bomb fell and was brought about by overwhelming maritime power ... Her shipping had been destroyed".[24] At the Potsdam conference, Stalin had already conveyed to Truman a message announcing the imminent arrival in Moscow of former Japanese Prime Minister, Prince Fumijaro Konoye, for talks on ending the war. An essential part of the message, conveyed to Truman 10 days before the nuclear massacres — and subsequently suppressed for 25 years by the US State Department — confirmed it was Emperor Hirohito's "earnest hope that peace may be restored as speedily as possible for the welfare of mankind".[25] Truman, despite his ostensible concern for "saving a million lives", rejected the prospect of a negotiated surrender. Bearing in mind that rejection, together with the West's clear aversion to the geo-political consequences of Soviet participation in the war against Japan, it can plausibly be concluded that Truman regarded the atomic bomb as the master key in future relations with Russia. The demonstrable superiority of Western air power would affect not only the outcome of Russia's territorial claims in the Far East, but also the vexing question of post-war boundaries in Europe.

One of the most cogent reasons for the West not using force on the ground in Europe was that military coercion of a foreign power to make it concede to political demands had traditionally required a long period of military operations and the defeat of that country's armed forces. But the armed forces of the Soviet Union, despite their heavy losses sustained during the war against Hitler, were now the world's greatest land power, stronger in men and conventional weapons than the combined forces of the US, Great Britain, Canada and France.[26] Stalin had 17 Red Army divisions deployed in Europe, in the Soviet zone of occupation behind the Iron Curtain, whereas the US Army in Germany had been drastically weakened by demobilisation and redeployment since the end of the war. Moreover, neither the British nor the French, heavily committed as they were to colonial wars and policing actions in other parts of the globe, were in a position to contemplate a new ground war in Europe so soon after the last one.

Atomic blackmail was meant to change all that. The Soviets were doubtless well aware that long-range American bombers of the type used at Hiroshima and Nagasaki were easily capable of flying deep into the USSR, carrying nuclear weapons. On September 22, 1949, however, the Russians successfully exploded their first atomic bomb and thus achieved nuclear parity with the West. Equilibrium of a kind was achieved, with the frontier between the two halves of Germany forming the front line of the Cold War in Europe.

Only the armaments manufacturers of the West's military-industrial complex would emerge any richer from the nuclear arms race that followed. Two different histories would co-exist side by side: a secret, conspiratorial history, censored and restricted, which nobody was supposed to be aware of, and a public chronicle based on mass deception, socially engineered arrest of consciousness, and cognitive and causative disorientation away from reality. This would be the West's dark side, a side the Cold War allowed our military and political leaders to keep hidden. They would discourage critical assessments of such matters as the politics of history and the integration of history into political transformation, thus evading an enlightened quality of historical interpretation. The official view would be that the history of the Cold War must be told on the basis of censored official documents, or not be told at all.

The word "democracy" would serve to imply the evil of socialism, and the supposed well-being of capitalism and of Western humanitarian crusades. It would somehow be offensive not to be a democrat. Anyone or anything suspected of not being democratic would be considered either subversive or pathological — while democracy conferred the right of democratic storm troopers to impose authoritarian rule wherever they chose, and in every corner of the globe.

Chapter 8:

Banishing the *'Banditti'*

When the Germans withdrew from Greece in October 1944, 10,000 exiled regular Greek soldiers mutinied in Cairo, demanding the resignation of the Greek government then exiled in Egypt, and the establishment of a socialist republic in Greece. The Allied high command promptly had them rounded up and transferred to concentration camps in Africa for the duration of the war. Churchill, himself a paragon of virtue, considered these erstwhile Greek allies to be "indistinguishable from *banditti*", and Greece could not be allowed to come under the control of Greeks who were "contaminated by revolutionary and communist elements".[1]

This "contamination" derived from the communist-led ELAS-EAM partisan movement whose guerrillas had substantially advanced the Allied cause in the Near East. The partisans had pinned down about 300,000 German troops, frustrated enemy plans for labour conscription, sabotaged German transportation, supply and communication networks, and rescued thousands of prisoners of war from the occupation forces. Those rescued included many Allied airmen who had been shot down.[2] On the political front, ELAS-EAM had also established socialist structures in the countryside — which was probably the reason why Britain's Special Operations Executive (SOE) had in the winter of 1943-44 terminated clandestine arms supplies to the communist-led guerrillas. SOE, in a manner reminiscent of identical moves in Malaya earlier, concurrently stepped up support for the rival EDES populist movement, which posed no post-war threat to capitalism and was confined to a small, inconsequential power base in Epirus.[3] Nevertheless, when the Germans finally withdrew from Greece, a communist-led insurgency was launched by ELAS-EAM against the right-wing Greek monarchy in Athens. The uprising was crushed in December 1944 by British forces. They promptly restored the old and manipulable Greek monarchy, plunging the country into civil war. Britain then withdrew its forces, the burden of "containment" having enthusiastically been taken up by the United States.

Washington quickly stepped up subsidies to the Greek pro-monarchist ruling elite — as also to Cyprus and Turkey. This US "aid" in the face of a "communist threat" was, however, simply a concrete issue of overt policy behind which to conduct a programme of covert intervention. Greece's entire social, political, military and economic structures became secretly planned, decided and executed by the American Mission in Greece. Greek civil liberties were eroded, the left wing of Greek politics was all but destroyed, pro-monarchist armed forces were greatly strengthened, the trade union movement completely undermined, and a rightward swing reinforced in Greek affairs as a whole.[4]

Pro-nazi Greeks, for their part, had hunted down many partisans and participated in the liquidation of about 70,000 Greek Jews during the war. By 1947, a group of like-minded individuals known as the Holy Bond of Greek Officers, or IDEA according to its Greek acronym, was the clandestine recipient of millions of dollars in aid from Washington. Enough money, arms and supplies were provided by the Americans to equip a fighting force of at least 15,000 men, which soon emerged as the dominant force in Greek affairs. This force, led by former Nazi collaborators, was deemed by Washington to be a "secret army reserve".[5] It was formed in terms of United States National

Security Council Directive NSC-10/2, which formalised the doctrine of covert action, allowing President Truman and successive American leaders to increasingly abuse their constitutional role. NSC-10/2 made it permissible for covert operations to be planned and executed in such a manner that any US Government responsibility for, or involvement in, those actions would not be evident to unauthorised persons and, if uncovered, the US Government could "plausibly disclaim" any responsibility for them.[6]

Leading IDEA members headed the armed forces while Colonel George Papadopoulos, the founder of IDEA, was promoted to head the new Greek central intelligence agency, the KYP, while Athens became the CIA's most important operational centre, serving as a springboard for all the CIA's Near East operations.[7] Former partisans were rewarded for their participation in the fight against fascism by having voluminous police files kept on them. Communism in Greece, explained US Secretary of State Dean Acheson, had the potential to "infect Iran and all countries to the east". It also threatened to "carry infection to Africa through Asia Minor and Egypt, and to Europe through Italy and France, already threatened by the strongest domestic communist parties in Western Europe."[8] No effort was spared in extolling the virtues of capitalism and the evils of Marxism. The Americans constructed a powerful radio broadcasting station in Salonika for the purpose of discrediting "Soviet expansionism" and extolling the moral superiority of democracy. The broadcasts somehow managed to overlook the fact that the United States had itself succeeded in imposing its own *Pax Americana* on Greece. During the war against Germany the USSR had not even materially supported the Greek partisans, who were backed primarily by Albania and Yugoslavia.[9]

The CIA's Office of Policy Co-ordination, flushed with its success in propping up a rightwing dictatorship in Greece, lost no time in underwriting a similar covert intervention in Italy, where the usefulness of communist-led partisans and left-wing labour activists had come to an abrupt end with the Allied landings in Sicily. As in Greece, relations between the Western Allies and the partisans rapidly turned full circle. The role in civil society of former partisans was quickly nullified by the Allied Military Government in Occupied Territories and by the Allied Control Commission, while leftists and liberal elements, particularly those in the Italian labour movement, were openly ostracised. Field Marshal Pietro Badoglio, Italy's former fascist Chief of General Staff and number one on the United Nations list of war criminals, was ceremoniously welcomed by the West as a "co-belligerent". His "honourable capitulation" from the Axis had been secured on the understanding that his past crimes would simply be wiped off the slate.[10]

Truman now evoked his country's War Powers Act to provide a reservoir of unvouchered funding for the purpose of rigging Italy's first post-war general election in 1948. In terms of the War Powers Act, the US government had authorised a Treasury Exchange Stabilisation Fund to "safeguard" captured Nazi currency, gold, precious metals, and stocks and bonds seized from Axis governments attempting to smuggle this wealth out of Europe during the war.[11] This tainted money was now used to fund covert operations in Italy where communists had formed the bulk of the Italian partisan forces during the war and represented a large section of the workers in northern Italy who had been mainly responsible for the fall of Mussolini.[12]

Past and present Nazi sympathisers, collaborationists and fascists were given far more political opportunities than the anti-fascists as preparations forged ahead in 1948 for the country's first post-war "democratic" election.[13] Two separate Italian labour movements had come into being in 1944: one largely Catholic and pro-American and the other largely communist. It was therefore not surprising that the good Catholic James Jesus Angleton had in 1945 headed the United

States' Office of Strategic Services in Rome. Angleton, destined later to become director of the CIA in Washington, had arranged with the Vatican under Pope Pius XII to receive information emanating from the Jesuits who had an unparalleled information-gathering service about Italian communist activity.[14] It is a measure of the importance with which Washington viewed Rome that when Angleton left Italy he was replaced by another good Catholic, William E Colby, destined later also to become a director of the CIA.

Such was the overall complexity and political sensitivity of the intricate web of contacts established during the war, between the Nazis and the Papacy, the Papacy and the United States, and secret contacts between all of them mediated by the Vatican Information Service, that it is unlikely the full story will ever be known. Undoubtedly, many Italian Catholics resisted Nazism during the war, frequently at great peril to themselves and sometimes at the cost of their lives. The British Legation within Vatican City was allowed to function during World War II despite the fact that it was running an Allied POW escape route from there.[15] The Pope either turned a blind eye to this or was unaware of what was going on. Whatever the truth of that matter, it is certainly the case that during the war Pope Pius XII had continually refused to condemn Nazism – earning for himself the nickname "Hitler's Pope".[16]

After the Germans secretly negotiated an early surrender with the Western Allies rather than surrender to the partisans in northern Italy, a Nazi refugee transit camp was established with the complicity of the American secret services. Through this camp about 5,000 Nazi fugitives – including such notables as Adolf Eichmann, Klaus Barbie and Walter Rauff — were assisted to flee abroad, mainly to South America, thus escaping prosecution for war crimes in Europe. Cardinal Siri, Bishop of Genoa was linked to this "humanitarian" project, as was Giovanni Battista Montini — the future Pope Paul VI – who was particularly well-placed to assist the fugitives. He had under his supervision not only the Vatican bureau that issued refugee travel documents, but also the Church's international welfare organisation Caritas Internationalis. [17]

The depth of Catholic anti-communist feeling during the run-up to the 1948 elections was such that the archbishops of Milan and Palermo announced Catholic communists would receive neither absolution nor confession. Anyone with communist affiliations could not even have a Christian burial nor be buried in holy grounds.[18] The CIA channelled large amounts of money to the Catholics to assist their ritual evocations of a ruthless Stalinist enemy hellbent on taking over the world. One leading Catholic figure alone — a Monsignor Don Giuseppe Bichieria of Milan — was provided with enough money to buy vehicles and weapons to support a vigilante group consisting of about 300 anti-communist Catholic youths whose function it was to assault leftwing candidates and break up meetings in their favour.[19] The effects of such strong-arm tactics combined with the general manipulation of political process and an unprecedented propaganda onslaught to result in a comfortable win for the Christian Democrats. It was of course lauded by the "free press" as a victory for democracy.

Ironically, the Atlantic Charter which Britain and America signed in 1941 to lure communist-led partisans to fight on their side, had essentially been a promise of freedom from despotic rule, and ostensibly a declaration of respect for "the right of all peoples to choose the form of government under which they will live". And while the labyrinthine round of media hype, mass deception, post-war betrayals, abandoned allegiances and covert manipulation of anti-communist attitudes and opinions might have come as a shock to leftists in Greece and Italy, there was in fact nothing new or even surprising about such wartime duplicity. The writing had already been on the wall six years earlier, in 1941, when Britain's SOE had discontinued its clandestine supply of arms to the communist-led guerrillas of the Malay People's Anti-Japanese Army (MPAJA). * SOE had then proceeded to train a rival, non-communist guerrilla force known as Force 136, recruited largely from among foreign, nationalist Chinese, and to all intents and purposes a mercenary force.[20]

Though the MPAJA and its parent organisation, the Malaya Communist Party suffered major setbacks in 1942 after the discontinuation of SOE arms supplies, they had managed against all odds to regroup their forces and operated in every Malay state, harassing the Japanese army of occupation with hit-and-run guerrilla warfare. By the end of the war the MPAJA mustered a total of about 4,000 guerrillas supported by tens of thousands of sympathisers.[21] The Malay communists, like their Greek and Italian counterparts who had advanced the Allied cause and were keen after the war to form governments of their own choice, were similarly betrayed by their erstwhile Western allies. But a very different set of geographical, cultural and historical factors prevailed in the Far East, allowing resistance to post-war foreign domination to be far more fierce in Malaya that it had been in either Greece or Italy. British and Commonwealth forces in Malaya would become embroiled in a bitter and prolonged counter-insurgency war

---

* The West also had a useful precedent dating back to the Sykes-Picot agreement of May 1916, a secret understanding concluded between Great Britain and France, for the dismemberment of the then Ottoman Empire, ruled by Turkey, a World War I ally of Germany. The agreement, taking its name from its negotiators, Sir Mark Sykes of Britain and Georges Picot of France, effectively reneged on pledges of a unified, post-war, independent Arab state. The pledges had been given by Britain to the Hashimite leader Husayn ibn Ali, Sharif of Mecca, to encourage him to lead an Arab revolt against the Turkish rulers of Syria, Iraq, and Lebanon. Palestine was to have been under international control. But, after the war, former Ottoman-ruled Syria, Iraq, and Lebanon were duplicitously divided into various French and British-administered areas, and Britain claimed Palestine as a British mandate, thus contributing to the origins of a bitter conflict that survives to this day. The World War I Arab revolt against Turkish rule is famously recounted by Colonel TE Lawrence, "Lawrence of Arabia", in his memoirs.

against their former anti-fascist allies. Nor did the endless round of betrayals, duplicity and broken promises of post-war freedom from colonialism end there. Elsewhere in the Far East, even before the ink had properly dried on the Japanese surrender agreement, Britain had swiftly transported fully armed Japanese troops to Indonesia, and also to Vietnam, where the Japanese were encouraged to fight with renewed vigour against the former, anti-Japanese resistance groups. In Indo-China, former French forces that had collaborated with the Axis were encouraged to stay on to fight the communist leader Ho Chi Minh. In the Philippines, America's oldest neo-colony, the Americans were similarly fighting their former communist allies.

In China the Western crusade against national self determination followed suit. The Commanding General of US Forces, General Albert C Wedemeyer noted that the post-war disarming of Japanese troops by the Chinese failed "to move smoothly" because fully armed Japanese forces were being employed to fight Mao Tse Tung's Chinese communists.[22] In Truman's words: "If we told the Japanese to lay down their arms immediately and march to the seaboard, the entire country would be taken over by the communists. We therefore had to take the unusual step of using the enemy as a garrison ..."[23]

In Korea, however, the communist guerrillas were having none of that. They had been fighting Japanese occupation since 1932 and throughout World War II without any help from the West. The only outside assistance they ever received was from the USSR when it entered the war against Japan on August 8, 1945 and swept down the Korean peninsula, driving the Japanese before them. It was only a month later that US troops started arriving in force. Nonetheless, on August 15, United States General Order No.1 had called for a US Army delegation to take the Japanese surrender in Korea south of the 38th parallel, splitting the country in two. The USSR accepted the division in silence, while Korean communists proceeded to establish their own government in Seoul, anchored in widespread "people's committees" in the countryside. The US reacted by shunning the rural committees and setting up a full military government with jurisdiction throughout Korea.[24]

Russia withdrew its troops soon after. In the period that followed, the United States stood accused of provocations and appeared determined to reunify the peninsula by force. In mid-1949 the United States refused to recognise the existence of the new communist regime in China, and the Soviet Union withdrew temporarily from the United Nations, in protest. The United States, taking advantage of the USSR's continued absence at the UN, swiftly convened the UN Security Council, obtaining from it within two days a resolution condemning China's entry into the conflict and ordering all UN members to help South Korea, which the Soviet Union, owing to its absence, could not veto.[25] Hostilities finally broke out on June 29, 1950 after many border incidents and the defection of two companies of South Koreans to the North. A US State Department team went to work the same night polishing up a resolution branding North Korea the aggressor, woke up UN Secretary-General Trygve Lie at 3:OOam, got Lie to call a Security Council meeting that day, and pushed through the resolution. No attempt was made to verify the truth of the matter independently.[26]

On October 8, China entered the Korean conflict on the side of North Korea, citing American provocations in the region. By the end of 1950 the troops of 30 Western countries were ranged against North Korea, thus effectively allowing an undeclared American war to be fought as a UN police action under American command. By the time all non-Korean forces were finally withdrawn from Korea five years later, the bloodbath would be measurable to the extent of at least a million Koreans dead and 33,500 Americans killed in the fighting. It was the price they had to pay for America having become locked into economic dependence on militarisation and on military confrontation to sustain its military-industrial complex.

The crucial National Security Council planning document NSC-68, issued just before the Korean war, had warned that the West would face "a decline in economic activity of serious proportions" without a government stimulus through increased military spending. NSC-68 served as the instrument with which Secretary of State Dean Acheson then bludgeoned the government into accepting an extensive re-militarisation of foreign policy in the aftermath of World War II.[27] The outbreak of war in Korea simply served to legitimise a huge United States military build-up already planned and in search of enemies to set it in motion. At the outbreak of war, US President Truman swiftly established a so-called Psychological Strategy Board (PSB) which co-ordinated a programme conforming in all essentials with what the Joint Chiefs of Staff recommended as "a large-scale programme of psychological warfare, including special operations, comparable in scope to the Manhattan (atomic bomb) project of World War II". PSB escalated accordingly the mobilisation of "an extensive co-ordinated program, already under way, of keeping the people of the United States informed as to the nature of the peril in which they stand and the measures required to avert it."[28]

When the American forces in Korea were forced into retreat through combined Chinese and North Korean numbers, Truman promptly stepped up the psychological offensive at home by appointing Charles E Wilson as "War Mobiliser". Wilson also just happened to be president of the General Electric Corporation, America's second largest military contractor, third biggest builder of nuclear weapons systems and, conveniently, owner of the National Broadcasting Corporation. He saw it as part of his function to explain to news editors that the role of news media was to "create and sustain a state of mind in the people, which is vital to the nation's mobilisation effort (because) the most vicious enemy of America today is the shocking apathy of the American people to the very real dangers of atomic attack on their cities and themselves."[29]

That China did not yet have an atomic bomb was apparently beside the point, and although the Soviet Union had by then successfully tested a nuclear weapon, it still lacked the necessary long-range aircraft with which to deliver such a bomb even if it might have wished to do so. The United States, by contrast, possessed not only an overwhelming nuclear weapons capability but it had also made significant advances in chemical and bacteriological warfare (CBW). During the period January to March 1952, at the height of the Korean war, US aircraft dropped vast quantities of bacteria and bacteria-laden insects over North Korea and north-east China in covert operations that would successfully be covered up for nearly three decades.[30]

Such weapons were banned in terms of a Geneva Protocol and the Biological Weapons Convention as well as international law. But then in October 1980, to considerable official dismay, the authoritative *Bulletin of Atomic Scientists* published a major and fully documented study in the United States, referring explicitly to America's ongoing collaboration with Japanese war criminals in the development of CBW. Many Russian, Chinese, American, British and Australian prisoners had been subjected to freezing, ballistics and vivisection experiments, and the research data was secretly exchanged by Japanese scientists in return for immunity from war crimes prosecution.[31]

The *Bulletin of Atomic Scientists* article set off a hornets' nest by reviving allegations dating back to the 1950s when the United States had first been confronted with Chinese allegations to this effect. Naturally the American leadership denied vehemently the existence and use of such weapons. The Chinese allegations were nonetheless corroborated a few months later by the International Scientific Committee (ISC), comprised of scientists from all the major industrialised countries. After deliberations lasting more than two months, the ISC concluded:

"The peoples of Korea and China have indeed been the objectives of bacteriological weapons. These have been employed by units of the USA armed forces, using a great variety of different methods for the purpose, some of which seem to be developments of those applied by the Japanese during the second world war."[32]

Elsewhere in the Far East, meanwhile, the CIA was busily financing its own secret wars through the proceeds of illegal drug running. From 1948 onwards, American intelligence activities in the "Golden Triangle" — stretching from southern Yunnan to neighbouring Burma's Shan states, northern Thailand and northern Laos — had been inextricably intertwined with the opium trade. According to author Alfred McCoy, in his definitive study *The Politics of Heroin in Southeast Asia*, the trade had first been established by the French in the 1880s to finance their colonial rule over Indochina. Nearly a century later the region was proving a major source of heroin destined for the American market. The region had throughout the Cold War been the launching pad for a multitude of US covert operations against China. Infiltration routes for CIA teams into southern China were also used as drug smuggling routes for traffickers in Burma and Thailand. Local Shan tribesmen provided guides both to the CIA's teams and to opium caravans near the Burma-Chinese border.[33]

The CIA front-company Air America would by 1968 have a fleet of several hundred aircraft of all kinds, operating out of six bases throughout Thailand and Long Tieng, the Agency's operational headquarters in northern Laos. Long Tieng was the main base of the Hmong commanding general, Vang Pao, and the site of his main heroin laboratory for the entire Golden Triangle region. In the late 1960s, the Agency even assisted Vang Pao in his purchase of Air America aircraft to form his own airline, Xieng Khouang Air Transport. The airline flew cargoes of opium and heroin between Long Tieng and Vientiane, the proceeds of which were then used to fund operations against the communists.[34]

Apart from its prowess in drug smuggling,[*] the CIA also had a significant psychological warfare capability. A US-backed nationalist Chinese "government in exile" having been installed in Taiwan under Chiang Kai-shek, the CIA operated powerful radio broadcasting stations on the island, posing as a clandestine broadcasting station within mainland communist China. To achieve credibility in its subversive propaganda beamed to the mainland, the bogus radio station combined disinformation with accurate information gleaned from genuine domestic Chinese broadcasts, all the while pretending the broadcasts were under internal dissident control. So convincing were the bogus transmissions that in the late 1940s and early 1950s some of the CIA's own media analysts and many academic researchers were completely taken in. This occurred frequently when the CIA department responsible for monitoring authentic Chinese broadcasts was not notified that some of the broadcasts it was listening to were in fact coming from the CIA's own bogus station. Even the CIA's own media analysts remained unaware that much of the material monitored had in fact been originated by the CIA itself.[35]

---

[*] By 1972 the CIA came under increasing pressure to prove it was not involved in opium and heroin smuggling for the Hmong mercenaries and drug-dealing generals in Indochina. The CIA was allowed to investigate itself by way of its own Inspector-General. Air America flew Drug Enforcement Agency agents to Southeast Asia "in search of the facts", and all parties came out of it satisfied the CIA was an honourable organisation. [See Christopher Robbins, *Air America: The Story of the CIA's Secret Airlines*, New York: Putnam's 1979, p.237, 239-40, n.13]. Senior CIA officers stationed in Thailand were later cited in the 1970s scandal around the collapse of Nugan Hand Bank in Australia. The bank was found to be heavily involved in drug trafficking between Thailand and Australia, as well as money laundering and weapons deals in South Africa and Asia. [See Commonwealth-New South Wales Joint Task Force on Drug Trafficking Report, Vol IV, (Part 2), Sydney: Government Printing Office, 1983].

This was just one consequence of the US government having coined the specific term "covert action", and assigned formal responsibility to the CIA for performing "any clandestine activity designed to influence foreign governments, events, organisations or persons in support of United States foreign policy". Another consequence was that by the early 1950s the CIA's covert operations abroad accounted for three-quarters of its budget, the intelligence agency having grown in size to six times its 1947 size.[36]

It marked the occasion by covertly arranging a *coup d'etat* in Iran before turning its attention towards Guatemala. No matter that both Iran and Guatemala were independent capitalist democracies without the slightest inclination toward Marxism; it was quite enough that they merely wished to pursue a non-aligned path. Guatemala was predictably compelled to turn towards the USSR for arms to defend itself, any form of assistance from the West being barred by US power. The CIA thus manipulated circumstances whereby, through the media, it was made to seem as though Guatemala posed a threat to US security. Next followed a series of covert interventions that destroyed Guatemala's independent economy, creating a situation conducive to a left-wing military coup which in turn "justified" an openly violent response from the US military.[37]

In Algeria, meanwhile, fanatical French right-wing army officers drew encouragement and inspiration from such methods. The seditious officers, including some who had collaborated with the Germans during the occupation of France, were anxious to avenge the total defeat of the French expeditionary corps by the communists in Indo-China and also the army's other humiliations in Morocco, Tunisia, and at Suez. They established for themselves a new role in the *Organisation de l'Armée Secrète* (OAS), a secret army supported by Algerians of European descent who were determined to retain Algeria under French colonial control. In their ranks were covert action specialists working for the

French army's 5th (Psychological Action) Bureau, and officers commanding French Foreign Legion and paratroop units in Algeria. Communist guerrilla warfare, according to them, did not have the objective of capturing strategic territory as in conventional warfare, but aimed to "conquer" the collective mind of the population through secret politico-military networks. So, from now on communism was to be fought on "equal terms", using the communists "own" methods and the systematic application of "*action psychologique*", terrorism, and a ruthless ensemble of clandestine techniques.

Some of these were modelled loosely on British counter-insurgency doctrine in Malaya during the 1950s when the British colonial authorities first recognised the importance of tying together civil and military measures into a single cohesive counter-insurgency policy. This included the selective "neutralising" of independence movement leaders, as quaintly referred to by the British Army's former Chief of General Staff, Brigadier-General Sir Frank Kitson, in his textbook *Low Intensity Operations*. Kitson also extolled the military advantages of making conditions "reasonably uncomfortable for the population as a whole, in order to provide an incentive for a return to normal life …" The Americans would later adapt that doctrine to their own "low-intensity operation" in South Vietnam, with the added refinement of a wide-scale political assassination program — the CIA's infamous Operation Phoenix. [38]

The self-styled counter-insurgency experts in Algeria seemed particularly impressed with Britain's use of "pseudo gangs" in Malaya — security forces posing as freedom fighters of the national liberation movement. The OAS adopted similar methods of deception, thereby attempting to alienate the masses from the liberation movement and conditioning them to accept State authority. Acts of terrorism committed by the OAS were falsely attributed to "the other side" and combined with the manipulation of opinion to create a climate of tension, anxiety and insecurity. The strategy collapsed after a failed 1958 military revolt in Algiers and a "general's putsch" in April 1961 which brought down the French government and threatened the political survival of its Gaullist successor, the Fifth Republic. Having failed to secure the "moral regeneration" of France many OAS members were forced to flee abroad, notably to Argentina and also to Portugal, where Lisbon became their strategic centre with official encouragement from the Portuguese secret police. In return for asylum and other incentives, battle-hardened OAS fugitives helped train foreign counter-insurgency and parallel police units forming the embryo of future "counter-terrorist" groups deployed around the world.[39]

Their exploits galvanised rightwing extremists everywhere, particularly so in Africa where repressive regimes plotted to destabilise and destroy nascent national liberation movements.[*] According to an internal report written in Lisbon by one OAS fugitive, OAS-inspired "counter-terrorism" units should bluntly endorse a "strategy of tension". This would work on public opinion and promote chaos, enabling right-wing provocateurs to later raise themselves up as "defenders" of the citizenry against the disintegration provoked by "leftist insurgency and terrorism". As one seasoned "counter-terrorist" warrior put it: "When you've got the masses by the balls, their hearts and minds follow."[40]

---

[*] British counter-insurgency doctrine in Malaya, as apparently adapted by the OAS, also served as a model for Rhodesian operations in Zimbabwe, and for South African death-squad activities during the apartheid era. On the origin of "pseudo gangs" as first used by Britain against the independence movement in Kenya see Frank Kitson, *Gangs and Counter-gangs*, London: Barrie and Rockliff, 1960. On Rhodesian pseudo-gangs see: David Martin and Phyllis Johnson, *The Struggle for Zimbabwe*, London: Faber 1981, pp.110-11; Ken Flower, *Serving Secretly*, London: John Murray 1987, pp.114-5. Rhodesian participation in Malaya is described in Christopher Owen, *The Rhodesian African Rifles*, London: Leo Cooper, 1970.

In early 1960s Europe, meanwhile, a similar mode of thought evidently failed to hold true in respect of an arsenal of intermediate-range nuclear missiles that the US had installed in Turkey, aimed at the heart of the Soviet Union. The Russians, with a nod of approval from Fidel Castro, promptly established their own missile site in Cuba, just 90 miles from the US mainland — resulting in what the "free press" conveniently dubbed the "Cuban missile crisis", which somehow failed to take into account the US's own missiles in Turkey. The stand-off was resolved when the US reluctantly agreed to remove its weapons of mass destruction from Turkey.

What remained firmly in place though, was the framework of US state propaganda. It was adopted without question, perhaps even without awareness, by the principal moulders of public opinion, the mass media.

Chapter 9:

Weapons of Mass Distraction

On the night of 4 August 1964, an urgent radio message was sent from Washington to the commander of warship *USS Maddox* on patrol off the coast of Vietnam in the Gulf of Tonkin. Washington wanted "confirmation" that the patrol had come under attack by North Vietnamese "aggressors". The commander of the *Maddox* was unable to supply the requested "confirmation", but still US President Lyndon Johnson went on the air shortly before midnight to announce the bombing of North Vietnam by American warplanes in response to aggression by the "other side". The media immediately voiced its support, describing the "attack" on a US warship as a humiliation that demanded reprisal. No matter that the presence of the naval patrol was itself highly provocative, there was no positive identification of any North Vietnamese vessel in the vicinity, and no American ship had been attacked.[1]

Seven months later, after repeated bombing raids failed to produce the desired results, CIA men quietly removed 100 tonnes of communist-made arms from a warehouse in the United States where they had been stockpiled for years. The agents loaded these arms onto a coastal boat, faked a firefight in which the boat was sunk in shallow water off the coast of Vietnam on February 16, 1965 and then invited Western journalists to see for themselves the "captured" weapons as "proof" that the war was covertly being fuelled by outside aid to the Vietcong.[2]

The Johnson administration then published its famous

White paper entitled "Aggression from the North". Accorded plenty of space in the mass media, the White Paper purported to be an account of the sinking of a "suspicious and carefully camouflaged vessel" moored off the coast of South Vietnam, where it was sunk "by the South Vietnamese forces". The White House noted that representatives of the free press visited the sunken "North Vietnamese ship" and viewed its cargo of Soviet-made weapons — "definitive evidence" of Soviet involvement in Vietnam. Hence the broad consensus of American public opinion was firmly behind the US administration when on 6 March 1965, just a week after the White Paper made its appearance, President Johnson ordered two US Marine Corps battalions to intervene openly.

Over the next 12 years, more than half a million American ground troops would be deployed in the rural regions of South Vietnam where 80 percent of the population lived and where, as in the case of Korea before, the political administration consisted essentially of syndicalist "people's committees". So, after the US government put in place a client regime in Saigon, the US Air began carpet-bombing rural South Vietnam to stem the "communist insurgency". The Americans would spray 72 million litres of concentrated herbicides across Vietnam, and they would bludgeon their opponents with three times the tonnage of bombs and far more artillery shells than the US armed forces had used against both Japan and Germany in all of World War II. The idea was to bombard on such a huge scale as to induce a mass migration of people from villages into cities, where they could be contained in refugee camps.

At least one prominent American academic approvingly described this as a process of "urbanisation". It would result in the slaughter of about 58,000 Americans and nearly three million Vietnamese, Cambodians and Laotians.[3] In the CIA's covert Phoenix Programme alone, death-squads posing as Viet Cong guerrillas would murder at least 20,000 pro-communist

Vietnamese, most of them civilians.[4] One general after another believed a combination of covert action and overt firepower would prevail, that a strategy of attrition and six million tonnes of bombs would grind the opponent down. And yet, America lost the war.

The US marked its defeat in Vietnam by propagating with renewed vigour the enhanced image of an implacable communist foe hell-bent on world domination. By then successive US administrations had, over a period of 25 years, demonised communism to such an extent that the threatening image they created was irreversible. That image assumed its own reality, defining the world in its own terms. It was a measure of the extent to which a subservient mass media could create a warped version of reality and of history. At a time when objective reporting was vital and could even have influenced the course of history, the contribution of journalists to public knowledge on matters of world importance was with only a few notable exceptions almost non-existent. The "Red peril" scare in many ways thus became a self-perpetuating myth at a time when the US itself was grossly violating international law.

Of the 900 major or sensitive CIA projects operating over the next two decades, media operations would form what an official US congressional investigation would later describe as "the largest single category of covert projects undertaken by the CIA". In just one year, 1964, the Pentagon spent $31-million on propaganda programmes devoted largely to publicising the "Red threat", in effect subsidising no less than 250 radio and 34 television stations. In Italy alone the CIA had by 1975 spent $75-million in covertly propping up the Christian Democrats and preventing the communists from gaining democratic control.[5] The CIA would remain a prime mover in bringing "stability" to at least 48 countries of the "post-war" world –but it would be "stability" at an extravagant price, bought at the cost of proxy wars, right-wing dictatorships, low-intensity conflicts, limited wars, secret wars, intervention, subversion and oppression within client nations, and the manipulation of consent at home. All this as a result of the legitimacy that had been conferred in the 1950s on the specific term "covert action", for which formal CIA responsibility was assigned in the performance of "any clandestine activity designed to influence foreign governments, events, organisations or persons in support of United States foreign policy".[6] Under the banner of "Christian principles" this meant trying to assassinate elected leaders such as Fidel Castro in Cuba, and supporting extremely violent right-wing coups as in Guatemala in 1954, and in fact creating all the military or right-wing dictatorships in Latin America, such as in Chile in 1973. The cost in lives was enormous: up to a million "insurgents" massacred in Indonesia in 1965[*]; 200,000 killed in East Timor in 1975; 300,000 dead in Central America since 1960; untold numbers killed in Angola; military coups in Argentina, Uruguay, Brazil and Chile — all inspired, engendered, subsidised and sustained to one degree or another by the US in "rolling back communism".[7]

The financial costs of replicating wartime methods of covert activity and subversive propaganda in "peacetime" were also enormous. The amounts of money then being poured into covert operations probably exceeding by far the entire budgets of many of the Third World countries targeted by the CIA. The political tenor of the day ensured that the "free press" exercised no real curiosity about the precise amounts and purposes of such funding.

Probably the most ambitious and expensive clandestine media project ever conceived by the CIA, however, was directed

---

* US State Department documents covering US assessments and policy towards Indonesia during this period are either closed to researchers or remain "missing" from official files. It took almost 25 years for the details of CIA complicity and the casualty figures of the Indonesian massacre to be eventually uncovered. See: *San Francisco Examiner,* May 20, 1990; *Washington Post,* May 20, 1990; *Boston Globe,* May 23, 1990.

not at the Third World but at eastern Europe. Under the auspices of a so-called National Committee for a Free Europe (NCFE) there came into being two radio broadcasting organisations — Radio Free Europe (RFE) and Radio Liberty (RL) — with their headquarters in New York and radio transmitters in West Germany. Officially registered as a charitable, tax-free non-government organisation funded by private donation, the objectives of NCFE were in reality far from charitable. The committee, under the personal tutelage of CIA deputy director Allen Dulles, was engaged specifically in subversive propaganda operations aimed at provoking a climate of dissent as the planned precursor to a general armed uprising behind Soviet lines. Upon taking up employment with RFE/RL,[*] employees were bound strictly to conceal their affiliations by signing the following pledge: "The undersigned has been informed that Radio Free Europe is a project of the CIA and that the CIA provides funds for operation of this organization. The undersigned has now been officially informed. If he divulges this information to a third party, he becomes liable for a fine and punishment not to exceed $10,000 and 10 years in prison."[8]

When RFE's transmissions first began in 1950, they were attributed to "freedom-loving East European exiles" speaking in their own languages and in familiar tones via their "very own" radio station. Men like "Colonel Bell", who was actually the author Ladislas Farago, broadcast on the airwaves of RFE every night. They pretended to be relaying "instructions" to an enormous army of agents in Eastern Europe — agents who really existed only in the recording studios of New York and in the fertile imaginations of CIA psychological warfare experts. When a train crashed or a fire was reported in the Eastern-bloc press,

---

[*] It was only in 1976 that Radio Free Europe and Radio Liberty merged formally into one corporation. For the sake of convenience they are jointly referred to here as RFE/RL.

RFE would broadcast congratulations to "saboteurs" on the success of their "latest mission". Stalinist repression tightened predictably in all the countries behind the Iron Curtain.[9]

The effects of these subversive propaganda broadcasts during the first half of the 1950s produced violent results in Hungary. By November 1956 at least 15,000 people, including about 3,000 Soviet soldiers, had died in fighting that broke out as the broadcasts pledged immediate international assistance to Hungarian rebels who were encouraged to rise in the mistaken belief that help was on the way.[10] Increased repression followed, after the uprising was eventually put down — the victims being those very same people whom the West had ostensibly promised to support. For the strategic deception to succeed, it was nonetheless essential not to impart any impression that the RFE/RL broadcasts were being conducted in the interests of a foreign power. Hence the use of unvouchered and untraceable funds emanating from the same reserve of captured German booty that had earlier been secretly tapped to rig the Italian elections.[11] Finding dedicated staff for RFE/RL was no problem. Around 500,000 East European exiles, including nearly 10,000 Nazi collaborators and many war criminals, had entered the United States after World War II under the Displaced Persons Act and the Refugee Relief Act.[12]

Among them were a number of propagandists who had worked for Hitler. Concentrated around RFE/RL were people like Yaroslav Stetsko, leader of the Organization of Ukrainian Nationalists (OUN). When the Nazis had occupied the Ukraine in 1942, Stetsko had proclaimed an OUN government in Lvov, responsible for the killing of thousands of Jews and whipping the local population into a frenzy of hatred for anyone suspected of communist sympathies. Other fugitives who had collaborated with the Nazis, as well as Yugoslav, Hungarian and other nationalist emigre organisations concealing their actual affiliations with the CIA, were now united into a solid alliance rallying around the Cold War banner raised by the West.[13]

The British secret service, never to be found lagging behind in such matters, made its own separate contribution aimed both at the Soviet Union and at the British nation itself, a large majority of whom had for a long time admired the USSR. When Tzarist tyranny was overthrown in 1917, word of the Russian revolution had come to the working class of Britain not as a social and political disaster but as one of the most emancipatory events in history. By 1948, because even more British people were singing the praises of the Soviet Union after its resounding victory over Nazism, the British government launched a double-edged weapon of mass deception that was directed as much at the British public as it was at the Soviet Union.

The innocuously named Information Research Department (IRD) was established in 1948, and its true function remained largely hidden from the British public for the next 32 years until British researcher Lyn Smith, in an astonishing paper published in 1980, shed light on IRD's inner workings.[14] Headed by a former member of Britain's wartime Political Warfare Executive (PWE), most of IRD's rationale and organisational structures were drawn from PWE — thus replicating in peacetime an organisation designed expressly for wartime strategic deception and perception management operations. Those of IRD's personnel not inherited from PWE were recruited from among East European emigre writers and journalists who were spared the tedious business of originating editorial material by themselves. All they had to do was lend their names to editorial material supplied by the British secret service. This IRD-generated material, attributed falsely to independent and well-informed sources, thus received a far greater degree of credibility than it might otherwise have done.

The only stipulations for the recipients of this subversive propaganda were that they could not attribute it to the government, the documents could not be directly quoted when used, nor could they be shown to anyone else, and the documents had to be destroyed when no longer needed.[15] Individual correspondents party to this neat little arrangement also included writers and reporters on all the major national newspapers.

IRD also made direct arrangements with several British newspapers, including *The Observer*, *The Times* and the *Sunday Times*, allowing them to select, reprint and distribute suitably pro-British and anti-Soviet articles provided by IRD for syndication and re-publication abroad. It was a strict condition of this agreement that the articles could not be altered in any way, nor could the official source be revealed, meaning in effect that a uniformly favourable image of Britain was disseminated abroad, deriving from the "independent" British press and hence apparently untainted by official bias. At the same time, MI5 and MI6 agents were planted on newspapers. Until 1959 the owners of the London *Sunday Times* allowed many of its foreign correspondents to co-operate fully with the British secret services during the Cold War.[16]

IRD's media operations extended themselves also to the British Trades Union Congress and to selected trades union journals which disseminated IRD-originated material. A supposedly independent right-wing magazine called Freedom First was subsidised heavily by IRD. The staffs of British missions and embassies abroad circulated IRD material to selected local media contacts while the BBC's external service transmitted IRD material to the world at large. At the same time, Britain's Labour government was plotting busily to "liberate countries within the Soviet orbit by any means short of war". British Foreign Secretary Ernest Bevin in particular hoped "to detach Albania ... by promoting civil discontent, internal confusion and possible strife". [17]

The Baltic states of Estonia, Latvia and Lithuania, less

than enthusiastic about their incorporation into the Soviet Union, had a thriving underground dissident movement. Believed by Britain to offer the best means for destabilising the USSR, it was this ready-made body of opposition that MI6 set out to harness with the help of exiles living in the West. British covert operations in the Baltic States, which began in 1944 against the Nazis, were escalated to include the recruitment and training in London of Balts, who were then landed on a Baltic beach by an experienced former Nazi naval captain. Their mission was to establish a pro-British spy network inside the Soviet Union centred on the Baltic States and stretching from Riga to Siberia.[18]

Red Army soldiers serving in Germany, according to IRD, comprised "a special category of listeners to the BBC's Russian service." It was to the BBC broadcasts in particular that IRD attached great importance, with the intention of encouraging disaffected Red Army personnel to defect. This, according to a top secret document of the time, was because "in the present state" of British intelligence about Russia, it was "vital for (Britain) to encourage defection, without which it is almost impossible to obtain the inside information which we so urgently need." In the event, however, only a handful of Russian soldiers defected — and then only in consequence of their relationships with German women. [19]

The need for intelligence about the Soviet Union was considered to be so pressing that Britain had little compunction about violating neutral Swedish waters when the Royal Navy landed a spying party on Russian soil and even penetrated into Leningrad harbour in the 1950s. An ex-serviceman who later confirmed his involvement in this operation was prosecuted under the Official Secrets Act when he published an article in the February 2, 1958 issue of the Oxford magazine *Isis*. His prosecution unwittingly provided official corroboration that the operation had in fact taken place. This was at a time when Britain was busily condemning the USSR at the United Nations for allegedly interfering in the affairs of other sovereign states, and the allegations were being repeated obligingly by the "free press". In condemning the communist "Iron Curtain" dividing Europe, Western politicians and journalists alike managed to turn a blind eye to history. The Soviet Union had never invaded any part of Europe except in answer to the Nazis and as a liberator The Red Army alone had ejected the German invaders from central and eastern Europe, thus achieving a presence in central Europe behind the Red Army's own military lines. All the territory behind Soviet lines at the end of World War II had been captured under internationally accepted rules of military engagement, and all those countries now under Soviet occupation had sent troops to fight on the side of Hitler — with the exception only of Poland.

Throughout history, however, Poland had been the corridor through which enemies swept into Russia — twice in less than three decades the Germans had passed through this corridor. In fact, since the beginning of the 19th century Russia had been invaded no less than five times: by Napoleon in 1812, by the British and French in 1854, by the Germans in 1914 to 1917, by the British and French again in 1918 to 1920, and by the Germans in 1941. With the Germans having been driven out of Poland by the Red Army it did not require any military genius to recognise that Stalin was not going to act hastily or against Russia's best interests with regard to post-war territorial gains in central and eastern Europe.

Nevertheless, the British and American secret services anticipated that a mass uprising in the Eastern bloc countries would occur if the existence of people there was made so intolerable that their daily misery exceeded by far the likely consequences of open dissent. The hardline Soviet security apparatus had already demonstrated its resolve in such matters when it massacred a large group of dissident Polish soldiers in the forest at Katyn during the closing stages of World War II. So, the plan was to provoke similar outrages on the part of the KGB, and to precipitate an intensified resurgence of repression reminiscent of the 1930s when, at the height of the Stalinist purges and show-trials, thousands of Russian dissidents were executed and another two million incarcerated in the notorious Gulag prison camps. That tragic episode had created a lasting climate of fear, suspicion and distrust in the USSR, which the West intended fully to exploit. It would force the Russians to choose options which, but for the covert manipulation of events by the West, the Russians would otherwise probably not have chosen.

Western disinformation experts, sparking off a renewed wave of Russian tyranny in the late 1940s and early 1950s, made sure Moscow received a constant stream of "evidence" that there were enemy agents and conspiracies against Stalin throughout the Eastern Bloc countries — Poland, Hungary, Bulgaria, Czechoslovakia, Rumania and East Germany. Coded radio messages that CIA agents knew for certain would be intercepted and deciphered by the Russians were sprinkled liberally with disinformation to the effect that there were domestic conspiracies against Stalin reaching into just about every sphere of East European life.[20]

In Munich, a subversive propaganda book-publishing house was established with covert US funding to produce agitative material throughout the 1950s. The CIA considered that "books differ from all other propaganda media, primarily because one single book can significantly change the reader's attitude and action to an extent unmatched by the impact of any other single medium."[21] Using the talents of former Nazi collaborationists, the CIA employed as the head of its Munich publishing house one Vladimir Porensky, a leading figure among East European fascists who had been imprisoned for war crimes in 1945. Porensky had been released just a year later with the co-operation of British intelligence. According to a declassified State

Department study, Porensky enjoyed the reputation of being a "200% Nazi".[22]

In the United States itself, the US Information Agency (USIA) funded a book-publishing programme in the late 1950s at an annual cost of $100,000, without American readers knowing that many of the ostensibly independent books they were buying and reading were in fact subsidised with their own tax money. When books condemning the "Red menace" did not meet commercial standards, USIA agreed obligingly in advance to eliminate the publisher's risk by surreptitiously buying up sufficient copies itself. USIA had in 1955 been incorporated into the Psychological Operations Co-ordinating Committee.[23]

Subversive broadcasting, however, remained by far the US's most expensive covert media investment. By 1973 the cost to American taxpayers of their country's subversive radio broadcasts abroad amounted to nearly half a billion dollars — the CIA's RFE/RL radio broadcasting outlets in Germany alone costing annually around $30-million. It was money well spent, according to one official US auditing report:

> ... the costs (of RFE/RL) cannot be considered separately from our nation's total cost of working for peace and deterring aggression. Over a long period of years, the contribution can obviate miliary expenditures many times greater than the broadcasting costs. Contrariwise, elimination of the radios could lead over time to increased military costs.[24]

The overall process of strategic deception was buttressed at home by the "free press" to the extent that it became difficult to tell when journalists were functioning legitimately or when they were acting in a State-sponsored capacity. Not only did many journalists regard the Cold War as "their" war, some also seemed to feel it as much their work to contribute to that war as to report it. In 1976 some of the most powerful organisations in American media and a total of around 400 individual journalists were implicated by an official US Congressional investigation into the CIA's covert relationships with the domestic media.[25]

Among organisations whose executives lent their co-operation to the CIA were Columbia Broadcasting System, *New York Times*, the American Broadcasting Company, the National Broadcasting Company, Associated Press, United Press International, Reuters, Hearst Newspapers, *Newsweek*, *Miami Herald*, *Saturday Evening Post*, *New York Herald Tribune* and *Time* magazine.[26] In short, both the British secret service and the CIA went in for "news" management in a big way. Disinformation was a large part of their strategic deception capability, and communists were not the only target of their lies. This was the golden age of deception and "plausible deniability". Bold operatives, functioning with almost limitless funds, were left to do as they pleased — as long as their leaders were free to deny it.

If there were dark secrets to be kept or dirty deeds to be done, most lawmakers did not even want to know about them. Congressional oversight of the CIA was essentially non-existent, and many reporters were more willing to spy for the Agency than expose its secrets.

By the 1980s, this widespread acceptance of covert activity, both inside and outside government, was no different. The only change, perhaps, was that since covert operations frequently involved breaking the laws of other countries, the secret services now thought they could break the laws of their own country and get away with it. A hawkish group of senior military officers formed a covert operational nerve-centre in the basement of the American White House. From there they ran what was in effect an independent, right-wing military-political organisation freer than ever from the burdens and constraints of public accountability or congressional oversight. Taking advantage of the White House imprimatur, this shadowy basement team could call on support, official and unofficial, from a range of personnel in the State and Defence departments. It could also call on the CIA, an underworld of retired generals and intelligence agents in the arms and security business, foreign mercenaries and a subversive propaganda machine that illegally corrupted the American press. Because the operation was "secret", President Ronald Reagan thought it would be easy for him plausibly to deny knowledge of the activities being planned and conducted in his basement. These included running a well-funded campaign to promote the Nicaraguan counter-revolutionaries or Contras as "freedom fighters", involving the misuse of public monies to the tune of about $600,000 a year. This was under cover of what US officials described as "a public diplomacy programme", and it violated entirely a US law preventing the American intelligence community from undertaking activities intended to "influence US political processes, public opinion, policies or media".

Senior CIA analyst Melvin Goodman later admitted at an official investigation into CIA-media activities that nearly every important allegation of Soviet terrorism that was asserted by the CIA in the 1980s — including claims of a Soviet plot to shoot the Pope — was "politicised", that is, not truthful.[27] Hence all the scare stories about non-existent squadrons of Soviet MIGs and a "Red Tide" sweeping up from central America to attack the US, each scare story tending to reinforce another and creating an illusion of multiple confirmation. A US government White Paper had also made its appearance, citing "definitive evidence" in its possession and consisting of about 80 captured guerrilla documents, portraying El Salvador as an area of East-West confrontation in which the US faced imminent dangers from the Soviet Union. Upon closer examination by independent observers the "evidence" turned out to be little more than clumsy forgeries. This did not prevent the Reagan administration from providing an immediate $25-million in aid to the rightwing dictatorship in El Salvador together with the provision of a further contingent of "military advisers" to reinforce those already there.

The Reagan years had got off to a good start when the first thing Reagan did on taking office in 1981 was to increase the "defence" budget by $50-billion, which subsequently rose by more than 50 percent between fiscal 1980 and fiscal 1985, when the Pentagon doubled the US defence budget — and tripled the national debt in the process. Attacks on "terrorist" targets were hence of great value, not only in vindicating past "defence" spending but also in enhancing the presentation to Congress of a case by the military hawks for even greater spending on new military equipment.

With "legitimacy" having been conferred by Reagan on the use of any methods in the war against "the axis of evil", it was not long before covert activity of all kinds became predominant forms of political behaviour throughout the Western society of nations, to be condemned only when the "other side" used them. Washington had in effect given a green light to all its allies in the Western orbit to escalate State-sponsored terrorism. In southern Africa, for instance, only a few hours after US Secretary of State Douglas Haig declared the "war against international terrorism" to be a top security priority for US foreign policy, South African commandos raided Mozambique and they stepped up military actions throughout the region. When South Africa invaded Angola in August 1981 the newly installed Reagan administration engaged in steady apologetics for this aggression and vetoed its condemnation in the UN Security Council. Official US statements held that the "incursion" — a relatively benign word that implied a modest and temporary intrusion — was "a defensive action against a Soviet-supported state".

South African agents also carried out sabotage and assassinations in Zimbabwe, and as the end of 1981 approached, an attempt was made to mount a coup against Zambian president

Kenneth Kaunda, and a major effort was made by South Africa to arm and support right-wing counter-revolutionaries in Mozambique. In 1983 alone, the consequences of foreign intervention and destabilisation combined with environmental factors in Mozambique to cause an estimated 100,000 civilian deaths and the displacement of one million people.

Pretoria also knew it could draw on the technical support of far-right organisations based in the United States. These included the Institute for Regional and International Studies (IRIS), headed by Robert D'Aubuisson, the former far-right president of El Salvador who was widely suspected of running death squads. IRIS was, and probably still is, closely linked with the World Anti-Communist League (WACL) — a Mexican-based neo-fascist group with branches around the world and drawing support from diverse elements in a loose consortium of the international ultra right. The function of IRIS, in the words of Major-General John K Singlaub, head of WACL, was to "provide technical assistance to those who ask for it and can't get it from government sources." [28]

In a letter on White House stationary read at WACL's 1984 conference, Reagan expressed warm greetings to all gathered. He observed that there were "eight active anti-communist resistance movements in every corner of the globe. All free people should stand in unity with those who risk their lives in the defence of liberty." And finally: "WACL has long played a leadership role in drawing attention to the gallant struggle now being waged by the true freedom fighters of our day."[29] The US had just been judged guilty of State terrorism by the International Court of Justice, for having covertly mined Nicaragua's harbours.

The world was already a dangerous place in September 1983, when American air-traffic controllers allowed Korean civilian aircraft KAL-007 with 269 people on board to stray deep into Russian airspace. The airliner, predictably mistaken by the

Russians for a military aircraft with hostile intentions in a militarily sensitive region, was then shot down by Russian MIGs when it failed to respond to warnings. Reagan was swift off the mark: "What can we think of a regime that so broadly trumpets its vision of peace and global disarmament", he asked, "and yet so quickly and so callously commits a terrorist act to sacrifice the lives of innocent human beings?" It was, explained Reagan, "an act of barbarism, born of a society which wantonly disregards individual rights and the value of human life and seeks constantly to expand to dominate other nations ... America must remain strong to preserve the peace ... we must maintain the strength to deter their aggression".[30]

Less than three weeks later the US House of Representatives voted by an overwhelming majority to allocate funds both for the nation's medium-range missile programme and for the production of binary nerve gas shells. Six weeks after that, it approved funds for further development of the strategic bomber programme. In both instances the destruction of the Korean airliner was acknowledged to be an overriding factor in determining the vote.[31] But then, in October 1986, a CIA transport plane crashed while ferrying illegal supplies to the right-wing counter-revolutionaries in Nicaragua. Reagan's days in the White House were numbered. On board the crashed plane was convincing evidence of high-level US government involvement in repeated arms shipments to the contras at a time when Congress had expressly forbidden it. Details started emerging about drug smuggling activities to fund unvouchered clandestine operations, and also about secret arms sales via Israel to the officially repugnant Iranian regime. Directed by Colonel Oliver North, the covert operations network with its nerve centre in Reagan's White House basement had moved profits from the one operation to the other via Swiss banking accounts not reflected in official US government "defence" spending audits.[32]

Suddenly the "free press" noticed a scandal.

Part Three

NEW WORLD DISORDER:
1991 — 2004

Chapter 10:

'Humanitarian' Crusades

With the rapid crumbling of the pre-World War II pattern of colonial relationships, a vacuum emerged which the United States deemed opportune to fill with US monopoly capital, which had gained strength during the war years. Washington moved from individual sporadic attempts to penetrate the colonies of West European powers to a planned and purposeful course aimed at expanding US spheres of influence and increasing its hegemony. In this endeavour the US had virtually unrivalled military and economic resources. In marked contrast to the Soviet Union, America had emerged richer, much richer, than any other nation involved in World War II. When the war ended, Washington controlled gold reserves of $20 billion, almost two-thirds the word's total of $33 billion.[1] Some major American corporations had even continued trading with Germany for the duration of the war. Standard Oil, for instance, had shipped enemy fuel through Switzerland for the German occupation forces in France; Ford trucks transported German troops; ITT helped supply Germany with rocket bombs and was also involved in building Focke-Wulf aircraft. The Chase, Rockefeller and Morgan banks had also been implicated in secret deals with the Nazis.[2]

Three decades later, "peacetime" economic growth in the US was being fuelled by a major and prolonged spurt in military spending on projects as such as "Star Wars". In just this one project, American taxpayers had during the 1980s forked out $4.5-billion annually in developing the capacity to reduce a modern medium-sized city to ruins within a just few minutes. Between 50 and 80 cents of every American tax dollar went towards supporting the military-industrial complex as the cost of manufacturing "conventional" US nuclear warheads and delivery systems rose by the late 1980s to an estimated $218-billion since Hiroshima. The US Department of Defence was linked to more than 100,000 contractors and subcontractors having branch offices in more than 100 countries in the Western bloc. Thousands of retired officers at the rank of major or higher, including admirals and generals, were employed by the top 100 military contractors who received the vast bulk of government military orders. Continually increasing "defence" spending was falsely attributed to a matching of increased military spending by the Soviet Union.[3] Since secrecy is the very antithesis of open debate, the CIA's budget during all this profligate spending remained a closely guarded secret. An informed guess by one former member of the US Senate Select Committee on Intelligence placed the CIA's in the mid-1980s at around $4.5-billion each year, "about a third" of which was spent on covert action.[4]

But a few years later the party was over. By the late 1980s, overall costs of the Stealth B-2 strategic bomber programme alone were amounting to nearly half the country's burgeoning $150-billion annual national deficit.[5] A general slowdown of the US economy together with a colossal budget deficit was forcing a reduction in "defence" spending and placing at risk millions of jobs. Unemployment was threatening the US on a scale reminiscent of the 1930s depression, and bankruptcy was threatening the US administration itself.

So, when the Berlin Wall came down, the American military-industrial complex was left flabbergasted and without coherent response other than to boost its already substantial domestic advertising. This advertising was not aimed at the army, navy or air force. They needed little convincing about the attractions of buying the latest in high-technology devastation. The advertising was aimed at the taxpayer and at the members of the Senate and House of Representatives who sanction weapons procurement programmes, and at a formidable voting constituency of around 6.5 million Americans who by late 1990 were on the payroll of military contractors or in direct Pentagon employment. A further three million workers provided related goods and services while the top 20 US defence firms had contracts with the Pentagon worth more than $1-billion a year each, being the beneficiaries of no fewer than 56,000 separate contracts handed out by the Pentagon each working day. [6]

Nevertheless, on January 2, 1991 the Council of Economic Advisers was forced to acknowledge officially that the country was in recession. US politicians, defence contractors and armaments budget negotiators — even with defence spending still set at around a staggering $300-billion for fiscal 1991 — were faced with bleak post-Cold War prospects. The US economy had been slowing dramatically for more than a year, US factories were operating at only 80 percent of capacity, the Federal budget deficit was well on its way to exceeding $200-billion, and the number of American people poor enough to qualify for food handouts had risen to more than 20 million. At the same time, large numbers of servicemen were returning from Germany now that the Cold War was "over". A deep recession and unemployment were getting worse, and the Pentagon was locked into a situation where the risks of cutting "defence" spending were both political and economic.

The end of the Cold War in the late 1980s and early 1990s thus precipitated a crisis in American capitalism. The collapse of the Soviet Union, initially celebrated as a victory, soon gave rise to a profound sense of uncertainty. The West had lost the "Evil Empire" against which it had defined itself for 40 years and asserted its global mission of "rolling back communism". So, the end of the Cold War now gave rise to a new term in the lexicon of human folly: "humanitarian intervention". With the end of the battles over territory and influence between West and East that defined the Cold War period, the US-led West would henceforth embark on a new global mission of "defending beleaguered peoples against ruthless dictators" and "upholding human rights everywhere". In so doing, the Western powers, and the US administration in particular, would project their domestic problems on to the world stage in an attempt to invest themselves with some kind of moral vision that was lacking in the domestic economic sphere.

President George Bush senior could not have asked for a better source of revenue than war in the Gulf when the Iraqi armies crossed the Kuwaiti border on 2 August 1990 in a bid to redress historical territorial claims to large chunks of what is now part of Kuwait. The scene was set for the daily flights of American B-52 long-range bombers taking off from British airfields during January and February 1991 to establish a new record, so proudly announced by the US-led coalition forces, for the greatest aerial bombardment in history. Within just a few weeks Iraq and its people sustained a tonnage of bombs almost greater than that dropped on Germany during World War II. In keeping with the "humanitarian ethos", this was heralded among other things as an attempt by US-led coalition forces to protect the Marsh Arabs in southern Iraq from Saddam's regime. America and Britain reiterated their war was most definitely not about oil, or national interests, or even personal vengeance. Rather, this was a disinterested war for the 'liberation' of oppressed people.

Nevertheless, the escalation of events leading up to the war had been contrived by the US in such a way as to cause Saddam to fall into Washington's hands and allow the Americans to do what they had always intended, but without alienating world opinion. Just four days before the Iraqi invasion, the US ambassador to Iraq, April Glaspie, told Saddam Hussein the US had "no opinion on Arab-Arab conflicts." This encouraged Iraq to invade Kuwait and put to destructive use all the heavy armaments the US and its allies had supplied to Saddam in the first place. In fact, just days before the Iraqi invasion of Kuwait, the Bush Administration had approved licences for $4.8-million in advanced technology products to Iraq.[7]

When news of the US victory against Iraq was announced six months later, the bomber barons of the military-industrial complex were overjoyed. The US military aircraft industry had been faced with cutting back on post-Cold War production. Military aircraft plants in particular were stuck with a problem of excess capacity and a need to find more overseas customers to maintain their industrial base. War in the Middle East solved that problem. Customers from across the Arab spectrum were suddenly beating a path to the American aircraft industry, seeking to buy the latest in winning weaponry that had just been proved under tough battle conditions. There were also huge profits to be had in the reconstruction of Kuwait reserved for American firms. The US Stock Exchange, after having languished for many months, suddenly saw the Dow Jones index soaring to strike the figure denoting a general economic upswing. Finance for most of this activity came from generous United Nations handouts and Kuwaiti borrowing against $50-billion in assets spread around the world.[8]

The biggest military build-up since World War II was not only lucrative. It paved the way for a permanent US military presence in the Gulf — close to the borders of the Soviet Union and to the soft underbelly of Europe. It also disclosed new features of post-Cold War military co-operation among NATO allies, taking place well outside the bloc's official zone of responsibility. Needless to say, this was all "in the cause of democracy". The US and its allies claimed moral justification for their military actions by persuading voters they were "making the world a safer place." Never mind nearly quarter of a million Iraqi dead; future conflicts with upstart "new Hitlers" promised to be rapid-paced and high-tech, entailing unrestrained use of the most sophisticated weapons – some of them actually banned by the United Nations. The US, having failed to reduce its economic dependence on military confrontation, was condemned to keep repeating that dependence, while humanitarian intervention was largely staged for a domestic audience, rather than being driven by any real concern for people around the world.

Successive US administrations, in attempting to impart some sense of moral purpose to their military escapades, would continue to rely on the dynamics that exist between secrecy, governance, the military-industrial complex, public opinion and the media. For most people in the West, post-Cold War support for "humanitarian intervention" in the 1990s was not a difficult decision to make. It was a means to assert some kind of moral purpose, and with the help of media the notion gained currency. The reality was that it conferred the "right of the international community" to overthrow sovereignty and usurp state authority in any nation where people could be portrayed by the media as downtrodden. Western elites would in this way continue to boost their domestic standing and distract attention from their domestic problems by "intervening selflessly" in the name of "humanitarianism". The war against Iraq would not be the only one to be located within this "humanitarian" ethos, and all this would be done as "a force for good" and "for advancing genuine democracy and human dignity" in all corners of the globe.

The West succeeded in justifying its interventions on the basis of ever-more selfless goals, in the name of defending the human rights of others Yet for those on the receiving end of this largesse, there was little that was humanitarian in these "'humanitarian wars". They contributed significantly to the 20th century being the bloodiest in human history.

In 1993, US forces launched their invasion of Somalia, catchingly named "Operation Restore Hope" — ostensibly carried out to protect Somalis from feuding warlords and poverty. There was a spectacular night landing of marines in front of TV cameras invited from all the major networks. But the marines with their night vision equipment were blinded by all the TV lighting, and the camera crews had to be ordered to withdraw from the beach. The invading marines, naturally, met with no resistance. Four thousand Somalis were subsequently killed by "peacekeepers" over a 12-month period — 700 people died on the night of September 5, 1993, alone. It served to deflect world attention from what was taking place in nearby Rwanda, where French intervention and US support for the rebel Rwandan Patriotic Front was to culminate in ethnic genocide to the extent of countless numbers killed.[*]

In the Balkans, meanwhile, old divisions were intensified, new divisions created, and thousands killed, after US-led "peacekeepers" occupied the former Yugoslav federal state. To this day, Yugoslavia's fragmented remnants languish under foreign military occupation or decline to the status of NATO client states. Western intervention in the Balkans after civil war there from 1992 to 1995 had encouraged secession among various regional players and the eventual rupture of the Yugoslav state. There was an upsurge of armed Islamic groups that fought against Serb forces on the Bosnian Muslim side, more or less becoming the law in a lawless land. As one report described it, in the war-torn and post-war Balkans, "a culture of lawlessness, abetted by a failed state, [took] root', creating ripe conditions for terrorist activity, as well as 'human trafficking, arms smuggling [and] narcotics distribution'."[9]

The reasons for a particular set of circumstances need not necessarily lie in one single cause, but certainly Western

---

[*] Estimates of the civilian death toll vary, from 500,000 to one million. [See Alan Kuperman, The Limits of Humanitarian Intervention: Genocide in Rwanda, Chicago: Brookings Institution Press, 2001.

"humanitarian" intervention was an important factor in the breakdown in ethnic relations in the former Yugoslavia. Western interference ruptured Yugoslavia's internal structures, while simultaneously ensuring external pressures were brought to bear on the region, the combined effects of which amounted to a process of destabilisation. By recognising the claims of separatist republics and groups in 1990 and 1991, Western powers — specifically the US, Britain, France and Germany — undermined government structures in Yugoslavia, inflamed tensions and heightened the potential for ethnic conflict. By offering logistical support to various sides during the war, and with the collapse of the Soviet deterrent having made British and American military power more threatening as a foreign policy instrument against those who contemplated local solutions to regional hostilities, Western intervention sustained the conflict into the mid-1990s. Many journalists, for their part, played a central role in calling for the arming of the Bosnian Muslims and for Western intervention on the side of the Muslims against the Serbs

After more than 7,000 Bosnian Muslims were slaughtered by the Bosnian Serb Army in Srebrenica during July 1995, Professor Cees Wiebes of Amsterdam University compiled a report entitled *Intelligence and the War in Bosnia*, in which he detailed a "secret alliance between the Pentagon and radical Islamist groups from the Middle East designed to assist the Bosnian Muslims." Srebrenica, in eastern Bosnia, had been under the "protection" of United Nations peacekeepers comprising a Dutch Army battalion when the enclave was attacked by the Bosnian Serb Army led by General Mladic.

Professor Wiebes's report, which formed part of the Dutch inquiry into the massacre, resulted in the resignation of the Dutch government. The report describes how, from 1992 to 1995, the Pentagon, in association with Turkey, Iran and "a range of radical Islamist groups, including Afghan *mujahidin* and the pro-Iranian Hezbollah", organised the movement of an "enormous volume of weapons" and eventually *mujahidin* fighters into Bosnia.[10]

The former Yugoslav states had sacrificed domestic policymaking for the promise of "Euro-Atlantic" integration. By the end of the decade, national policy and legislation in the former Yugoslavia was openly formulated and implemented by the West — without being mediated through the democratic process which the West itself constantly espoused. The Rambouillet Agreement in 1999, for example, attempted to impose a US State Department solution on Serb-Albanian relations rather than allow a compromise position to be freely negotiated by the parties. Under the terms of this "stability pact", much of national policymaking in the former Yugoslav states was annexed by Western-dominated international bureaucracies such as NATO, the World Bank and International Monetary Fund.

The fragile Bosnian state, in particular, was the product of international interference, which imposed the borders of a state that over half of the population, the Bosnian Croats and Bosnian Serbs, felt little allegiance to. This lack of legitimacy meant the constitutional framework and trappings of sovereignty such as the national emblem, currency and passports, all had to be imposed from without. To this day, Bosnia-Herzegovina has a UN High Representative who has unlimited authority to overrule all of the democratic institutions of a sovereign member state of the United Nations.

Meanwhile, the "stability pact", which was put together under the Clinton administration, assured the end of a multiethnic Kosovo in March 1999 when an estimated 2,000 civilians and 600 military personnel were killed by NATO bombs dropped from British and American warplanes onto the "international protectorate" of Kosovo.[11] All this in the name of "protecting a beleaguered people" and "removing the brutal dictator Slobodan Milosevic." — as if two wrongs could make a right.

Western intervention also had deadly and destructive consequences in Afghanistan, where American and British officials argued similarly that their invasion of the country in 2001 was in the humanitarian interests of the local peoples. Far from bringing peace and stability to Afghanistan, the International Security Assistance Force's routing of the democratically elected Taliban government effectively reduced most of the country to bandit territory run by mediaeval warlords. The Western media, for the most part, in loyally disseminating the humanitarian myth and notions of a "war against terrorism", remained uninformed and unperturbed by historical reality.

Throughout the 1990s, far from demobilising and trying to generate a peace dividend after the Cold War ended, successive US governments including the Clinton administration had done everything in their power to shore up America's Cold War structures in Asia and expand its empire of military bases into the oil-rich Middle East and the Persian Gulf. Imported oil makes up about 40 percent of the total amount of fuel consumed in the US which had long harboured a sense of vulnerability growing out of its excessive dependence upon foreign sources of energy. Thus, in April 1978 when the former Communist Party of Afghanistan now known as the People's Democratic Party of Afghanistan (PDPA) had seized power in Kabul, America's problems of energy resources intertwined with its geo-strategic concerns.

Former Afghan president Daoud had tried to eliminate the PDPA in the Spring of 1978 by arresting its leaders. That triggered a *coup d'etat* the next day when an armoured brigade took over the presidential palace and killed everyone inside. Three days later the Democratic Republic of Afghanistan was declared. The ruling PDPA immediately began to introduce extensive reforms and to establish closer relations with the neighbouring Soviet Union. This was not a cause for celebration in Washington. Among other things, the PDPA's take-over opened a way for the Soviet Union to gain convenient access to the warm waters of the Middle East, and it signalled a change in the regional balance of power. Just a year later, however, shaken by peasant revolts, urban upheavals and bloody internal feuding — much of it covertly sponsored by the CIA — the socialist regime was on the verge of collapse. On December 27, 1979 the Soviet Union intervened in terms of a security and co-operation agreement signed in December 1978 between Moscow and Kabul. Naturally, the Western media promptly labelled this intervention "an invasion". Only the West was permitted to do such things, and then it was legitimised as "humanitarian intervention" or "peace-keeping".

Although Moscow had not participated directly in the April 1978 revolution, there was a long history of cordial relations between Russia and Afghanistan dating back to the Moscow-Kabul Agreement of 1921. Still, more than half a century later, Soviet military power was suddenly portrayed as being on the move and posing a potential threat in the region. The US reacted harshly. It suspended sales of grain and technology to the Soviet Union, and also boycotted the 1980 Olympics, held in Moscow. At the behest of the West, the UN Security Council condemned the "invasion" and regularly called on the Soviets to withdraw. They did not.

So, on January 9, 1980, in Room S-407 on the Senate side of the Capitol, a confidential meeting took place between officials of the US Senate and CIA offers. On the agenda was a single item — a presentation by the CIA of its plans for covert paramilitary operations in Afghanistan. The senators offered no major objections. The next day CIA deputy director Frank C Carlucci advised the White House of the result of the meeting, and President Carter signed a Presidential Decision setting in motion a "secret" war against Afghanistan. This operation was secret only in name, news of its authorisation soon leaking out via reporter Ted Szulc of *The New York Times*.[12] What remained unreported, however, was that the US senators were merely acceding to accomplished fact. Clandestine CIA operations against Afghanistan had in fact commenced fully six years earlier.[13] That was soon after the Arab-Israeli war of 1973, when an Arab oil embargo was imposed on a number of Western countries that had supported Israel. The embargo had proved the important effects that developments in the Middle East region could have on the economies of Western nations — particularly the US, which consumes roughly 25 percent of the world's fossil fuels, while constituting only five percent of the world's population.

A geo-strategic pattern had in fact started emerging much earlier, with the CIA intervention against the government of Iran in 1953, when the US overthrew an elected government and installed a puppet regime there in the interests of the British and American petroleum industries. It had also failed to exercise its diplomatic muscle at the UN in 1956 when Britain, France and Israel attacked Egypt to prevent it from nationalising the strategic Suez canal. Since then, nearly all of the world's principal trouble spots were either in the centre of the main oil-extracting regions or near them.

After the fall of the pro-American Iranian monarchy in 1979, the United States sharply increased its military presence in the Persian Gulf region where Iran's oil deposits were estimated at more than 6,000 million tons, and approximately another 50,000 million tons were estimated in other Gulf countries. Lebanon, although having no oil deposits of its own, provided the shortest route to the West for the transportation of Gulf oil, principally from Iraq which has the world's second largest known oil reserves. So, Lebanon became a target for US "peace-keeping" operations in 1983 when American warships shelled Beirut and its surrounding villages with long-range guns. In Libya, with confirmed oil deposits of about 3,000 million tons, the

Americans were trying to kill Muammar Gaddafi for threatening US interests. They succeeded only in killing Gaddafi's six-year-old daughter. A crisis point was reached in the spring of 1986 when US carrier-based aircraft attacked Libyan vessels and bombed civilian districts in Tripoli and Benghazi.

In far-off Grenada, meanwhile, American marines had invaded the tiny island state and installed a puppet regime subservient to the US. Grenada's singular distinction is its proximity to Venezuela, the world's fourth largest and the largest producer of oil in South America, with known oil deposits amounting to about 4,000 million tons — about as much as the estimated deposits of the US today. Grenada also opens the way from the east into the Caribbean Sea, which washes the coast of Mexico, with a potential of nearly 7,000 million tons, one of the western hemisphere's largest oil reservoirs.

Those three regions — the Gulf, North Africa, and Latin America — within the sphere of diplomatic pressure and direct military intervention on the part of the US, give access to a total of 67,000 million tons of oil. This is nearly 80 percent of the known deposits of the non-socialist world, and their exploitation satisfies two-thirds of that world's requirements for oil and fuel. But oil is a non-renewable resource, and experts predict that by the year 2010, if not sooner, the supply of oil energy will begin an irreversible decline, along with a corresponding irreversible increase in price, despite growing demand from industrialised and developing nations.[14] Despite various claims by environmental groups, there is simply no readily available substitute for oil regarding transportation, nor do the alternatives produce the power output of oil. Hence a potential for future global "oil wars". The CIA and the White House greeted the April 1978 revolution in Afghanistan with particular hostility because of such potential, and because the revolution disrupted America's long-term, geo-strategic plans and imperial ambitions of dominating the Gulf region as a sphere of US influence.

Moreover, the PDPA was the first party in the history of Afghanistan to put forward a convincing programme for the elimination of lawlessness and poverty in the country. The PDPA sought to attain broadly democratic objectives including an end to large-scale land ownership and the redistribution of land to the poorest peasants; and to raise the population's general standard of living — in short, a socialist programme that was anathema to fundamental capitalist precepts of "the free market". At the same time, while the objectives of the PDPA appealed to the interests of the broadest range of the Afghan population, they caused fear and loathing among the feudal lords and reactionary priests. Feudal lords in pre-revolutionary Afghanistan controlled stock in banking, finance and commerce, and owned vast tracts of land and real estate.

Some were also spiritual leaders and heads of large family clans. They had been members of parliament, had formed the higher echelons of the pre-revolutionary government apparatus and judiciary system, and as such were a conservative force vigorously opposed to socialism. After the revolution, their numbers were strengthened by classes and strata on whose interests the revolution impinged: moneylenders, former government officials, discharged army and police officers, and land-owners. Of particular significance were the Islamic Party of Afghanistan, Jamiat-e-Islami, and a party calling itself Moslem Brothers, which were fundamentalist organisations set up by the higher clergy with the objective of promoting unequivocal submission to Islamic spiritual authorities and dogmas. Its members were violently opposed to leftists, and with the help of the CIA they set about forming guerrilla bands to engage in internal counter-revolutionary activities.

As part of its operations against Afghanistan during the Reagan administration, the CIA set up a regional headquarters in Peshawar, where it enjoyed the patronage of Pakistan's despotic, pro-Western military ruler General Zia-ul-Haq. The CIA then lost no time in establishing some 30 special camps and 50 bases along the Pakistan border, for training counter-revolutionaries or *mujahidin.** It was impossible for a clandestine operation of this size to remain secret for long. Soon independent sections of the Indian media, notably the publications *Blitz* and *Link*, reported that the *mujahidin* were being supplied with and trained in the use of sophisticated American weaponry including rapid-firing mortars and surface-to-air missiles. A steady flow of *mujahidin* recruits was achieved by the persuasive calibre of propaganda broadcasts by the so-called Voice of Free Afghanistan, funded by the US Information Agency. By the end of 1979 about 40,000 CIA-trained and equipped *mujahidin* were operating in Afghan territory.[15]

Needless to say, at the centre of the *mujahidin* leadership were members of the priesthood, whose influence was strongest in the Afghan countryside. In the years of struggle against the British Crown, many among the Mullahs had organised armed detachments and won great respect among the rural people, and before the April 1978 revolution, the local Mullah was village elder, teacher, judge, and ideologue combined in one person. They were the first to have been approached by the CIA, and a significant part of the lower, middle and higher echelons of the priesthood and their fervent followers enthusiastically joined the counter-revolution. From all corners of the Muslim world, young radicals flocked to Afghanistan to fight the Soviet infidels and drive them from the country of their Muslim brothers.

America poured funds into the fight, to the tune of more than $2-billion, and during the course of the next 10 years, the US through its surrogate, *mujahidin* forces, attempted to bleed the Soviet Union dry. After the Red Army eventually withdrew in 1992, a *mujahidin* coalition took power, followed by the US decision to abandon Afghanistan, thereby creating a power

---

* From the Arabic word *jahada*, meaning to strive, struggle.

vacuum that fuelled a war between warlords at the cost of tens of thousands of lives.

In the fullness of time, the unholy alliance between the US and radical Islam would have dire consequences for America. Among the *mujahidin* that the CIA had sponsored was a Saudi Arabian-born jihadist by the name of Osama bin-Laden.

Chapter 11:

The Haunting of America

In the aftermath of the September 11, 2001 terrorist attacks that claimed 3,000 American lives in New York and Washington, US National Security Adviser Condoleeza Rice called a hurried Press conference. She declared: "I don't think anybody could have predicted that these people would take an airplane and slam it into the World Trade Centre, take another one and slam it into the Pentagon, that they would try to use an airplane as a missile."

This alleged unpredictability of the attacks seems somewhat odd, given that Rice herself had been the top National Security official with Bush at the July 2001 G-8 summit in Genoa, Italy, where US officials were warned that Islamic terrorists might attempt to crash an airliner into the summit premises in Genoa. So seriously had Italian officials taken the threat that they closed the airspace over Genoa and positioned anti-aircraft guns at the city's airport. Perhaps the Americans, unlike the Italians, had felt so sure of themselves, so cloistered from any sense of possible retribution for their foreign military exploits, that they really thought they were immune to attack at home. Or perhaps there was a more sinister explanation: that available intelligence warning of the attacks had simply been ignored.

Whatever the truth of the matter, it is certainly the case that the September 11 attacks in Washington and New York were swiftly attributed by US officials to a shadowy network called al-Qaeda led by Osama bin-Laden. The earlier role of the

CIA in actively supporting such people was studiously avoided.

In their reaction to the atrocities, the perceptions of most Americans became so confused by official lies and distortions that a majority believed Saddam Hussein was the one behind it, even though there was no evidence that he could possibly have been. It was virtually taboo to ask what were the motives of the attackers, or if Saddam and bin-Laden were even distinguishable from one another.

False public perceptions were strengthened by Washington conferring the name "al-Qaeda" on the organisation supposedly behind the attacks — as though it was a conventionally structured organisation with a clear-cut chain of communication, control and command; a clearly definable entity that could be defeated by conventional military means. All that was needed apparently was to capture a few radical Islamists, eliminate a finite group of innate murderers and evildoers, and everything would be back to normal. It was this static view by US officials and the media that inspired the public's misunderstanding of Islamic terror groups. As a result, "al-Qaeda" was turned into something it is not. It is largely the creation of Western security officials who thought up a convenient label for an ubiquitous organisation having no formal name.

The label also helped obscure the CIA's historical relationship with the *mujahidin*, out of which "al-Qaeda" was born.[1]

The "al-Qaeda terror network" is in fact a loose collection or coalition of groups and individuals who do not even refer to themselves as al-Qaeda. They represent a radical, global ideology that has not only attracted many diverse individuals and regional groups, but has also facilitated a world-wide boom of new organisations that embrace identical thinking. By giving bin-Laden and his henchmen a name, Western officials had

unwittingly turned "al-Qaeda" into a symbol of heroic defiance.[*]
They also inflated it grossly out of proportion by making
unsubstantiated statements about the group's access to "weapons
of mass destruction", and by falsely linking al-Qaeda to Iraq and
Saddam Hussein.

In that way a persuasive *casus belli* was created for the
invasion of Iraq. But first Bush and the Pentagon needed a pre-
invasion staging post close to Iraq. This they attained on October
7, 2001 when US forces invaded Afghanistan and overthrew the
Taliban government in Kabul, which was allegedly providing aid
and succour to Osmana bin Laden and "al-Qaeda". By the end of
2001, however, the Taliban and "al-Qaeda" had retreated into the
countryside while the US-led armies of the Northern Alliance,
supported by American airpower and Special Forces troops, held
only the capital. About 1,000 Afghan civilians were killed by US
bombing and by other means, while US Defence Secretary
Donald Rumsfeld routinely responded to criticism about civilian
casualties by stating that "some amount of collateral damage is
inevitable in war." Taliban and former *mujahidin* "al-Qaeda"
fighters operated in small cells, emerging only to lay land mines
and launch night-time rocket attacks before disappearing again.[2]

The US's much lauded "victory" in Afghanistan was thus
not a victory at all. It was a campaign that effectively destroyed
the Taliban but failed to achieve the primary military objective of
ensuring that "al-Qaeda" could no longer operate in Afghanistan.
Despite the triumphalism of their media statements, the US-led
forces had succeeded only in driving the Taliban away from the
major cities, like Kandahar and Kabul, and into the rugged

---

[*] The only name ever used by captured Islamist terrorists themselves
was the World Islamic Front for the Struggle Against Jews and Crusaders.
According to British journalist Jason Burke, the term was first used by bin
Laden's spiritual mentor Abdullah Azzam, who in 1988 wrote of "al Qaeda
al Sulbah", meaning the "solid base". (Jason Burke, *Al-Qaeda: Casting a
Shadow of Terror,* London: IB Tauris, 2003).

countryside. Afghanis had always fought by retreating — in the face of the British colonialists in the 1930s, and farther back in the case of Alexander the Great — and then fighting a protracted war of insurgency.

The high point of the American involvement in Afghanistan came in December 2001, at a conference of various Afghan factions held in Bonn, when the Bush Administration's candidate, Hamid Karzai, was named chairman of an interim government. His appointment as President of Afghanistan was confirmed six months later at a carefully orchestrated Afghan "tribal council". There was no agreement on procedures for collecting taxes, no strategy for disarming either the many militias or individual Afghans, no resolution with the Taliban, and no trace of bin Laden or "al-Qaeda". Within a few months of the Bonn conference, as the US began its military build-up in the Gulf, security and political conditions deteriorated throughout Afghanistan. The conditions under which the post-Taliban government came to power gave warlords, bandits, opium producers and drug smugglers a new lease of life in the south and the east of Afghanistan, including the areas bordering Pakistan, which are *de facto* stateless areas insofar as there is no central control.[3]

Formal investigations, in the meantime, did little to shed light on the September 11 terror attacks that had served to justify the US-led invasion of Afghanistan. In July 2002, a House and Senate intelligence committees' joint investigation somehow managed to ignore the long history of US policies underlying the covert US funding of Islamic terrorists in Afghanistan. Nor did any journalist pick up the question or challenge the way the investigation framed its terms of reference. No-one questioned the way America's invasion of Afghanistan had magnified on a grand scale the conditions that Islamic militants found so provoking -- an unwelcome foreign presence in lands deemed sacred by Muslims. No-one even so much as hinted that the outpouring of anti-American feeling was not a sudden explosion, that it was, instead, the result of a long series of actions and reactions between the West and increasingly organised and determined international Islamic militias. The most important single event in this genesis may have been the September 11 attack, but the writing had been on the wall for a long time, and popular feeling in the Muslim world was that the Americans had it coming to them.

Be that as it may, the House and Senate joint intelligence committee's initial report in September 2002 disclosed that on several occasions starting in the mid-1990s, the CIA had access to information concerning the possibility of Islamic terrorists using passenger jets as *kamikaze* weapons against American targets. CIA chief George Tenet, using his power to declare information classified, refused to allow the intelligence committees to say whether a July 2001 briefing to "senior government officials" -- which reported that Osama bin Laden "will launch a significant terrorist attack" against the United States that "will be spectacular and designed to inflict mass casualties" — was actually delivered to Bush. The joint-committee further reported there were "numerous opportunities" during the tracking of at least two suspected Arab terrorists "when the CIA should have alerted the FBI and other US law enforcement authorities to the probability that these individuals either were or would soon be in the United States. That was not done."

In late March and early April 2004, a phalanx of top US officials was again ordered to answer questions at a US congressional commission of inquiry, formally known as the National Commission on Terrorist Attacks Upon the United States. This was ostensibly an inquiry into the Bush administration's handling of Islamic terrorism before the events of September 11, 2001. The historical links between the CIA and the Afghan *mujahidin* were again notably absent from the inquiry's terms of reference. Also conspicuously absent from the public hearings were President Bush and Vice-President Cheney — the two officials the public most wanted to answer outstanding questions. The absence of Bush and his inner circle at the public hearings was unsurprising, given that they had earlier tried to prevent any serious investigation of what happened on September 11, 2001. Both the president and his vice-president, while eager to invoke September 11 on behalf of an unrelated war, had warned Congress against an independent investigation of the circumstances leading up to the disaster. After public clamour for an investigation finally prevailed, the White House tried every conceivable tactic to hinder the commission, even while claiming to support it unreservedly.

In the event, it soon became clear that the commission would not ask all the questions that needed to be answered, especially in relation to conspicuous gaps and inconsistencies in the Bush administration's official submissions to the inquiry.[4] Certainly, nothing was said of the estimated 12,500 foreign *mujahidin* fighters who were trained in bomb-making, sabotage and guerrilla warfare in Afghan camps that the CIA had helped to set up. The commission thus achieved little to shed fresh light or dispel growing speculation that the Bush administration, which used an attack by Islamic fundamentalists to justify the invasion of Iraq, and which had been utterly ruthless in its political exploitation of September 11, ignored specific intelligence warnings prior to September 11, and in so doing, created circumstances conducive to such an attack.

Mainly, however, the commission was notable for its terms of reference having studiously evaded one key question: what were the reasons behind the attacks? No-one dared mention any probable motive arising from Arab frustration and anger against outside forces that had for many years interfered in Arab affairs, whether those forces were in the form of old-style British and French colonialism or, since World War II, naked US imperialism. More than 50 years of constant American intervention — whether in Iran or Iraq, Egypt or Jordan, Lebanon or Syria, Saudi Arabia or Yemen, Oman or Kuwait, or across the Red Sea in Sudan, Eritrea and Ethiopia —had ensured Arab disunity; a deep sense of frustration, and anger against the West.

Among other things, the White House had ordered the CIA to overthrow democratically-elected progressive governments, as in Iran in 1953 when left-leaning president Muhammad Mossadegh was dispatched. The result was a quarter-century of repressive rule by the Shah of Iran, a US puppet finally overthrown by Shi'ite fundamentalists, who established another repressive regime. The reason that only religious fanatics were in a position to seize power was that Iran's secular left and democratic forces had been killed, imprisoned or exiled by the Shah, with US approval. In Iraq, the CIA had repeatedly intervened from 1958, when progressive General Abdul Karim Kassem overthrew the British-installed monarchy, until 1963 when he was overthrown with US help. Many thousands of leftists and communists were killed along with Kassem. This ultimately led to rule by the secular and at the time pan-Arab Ba'ath regime. In 1979, General Saddam Hussein gained control of the Ba'athist government, purged and killed any remaining leftists, and within a year launched an unjust war against Iran that was unequivocally supported by Washington before ending in stalemate in 1988.

The refusal of Bush and his inner circle to testify in public at the National Commission on Terrorist Attacks Upon the United States was remarkable for the fact that world attention and great public interest were focussed on Bush's professed "war against terrorism". The deliberate crashing of two hi-jacked airliners into the World Trade Centre in New York, and a third into the Pentagon building in Washington, had been one of the most widely reported events in modern history since Pearl

Harbor. Yet, as with Pearl Harbor, there has to this day never been an open and honest accounting of the full circumstances surrounding or leading to what took place, nor did the media generally excel themselves in pursuit of the truth. Poorly documented or entirely speculative claims of a dire threat from Iraq received prominent, uncritical coverage, while contrary evidence was either ignored or played down. Still, one thing is indisputable: the events of September 11, 2001 were the unintended consequences of clandestine policies and practices that had for years been kept secret from both the American public and the world at large, and of which many ordinary folk continue to be unaware.

The available and largely unpublicised evidence suggests strongly the events of September 11 were not seen by Bush and his inner circle as an avoidable tragedy but as an opportunity, and the US administration was pushing a series of foreign policy objectives that it had before September 11. These were not defensive, but offensive goals -- ones that involve expanding US economic and military power abroad. Bush's real agenda may have had nothing to do with fighting terrorism or reducing its likelihood, but was concerned rather more with the cultivation of a national attitude of vengeful victimhood, an attitude the Bush administration actively promoted for its own benefit and political protection. With the attacks on the World Trade Centre and the Pentagon, a critical constraint was lifted — the constraint of public opinion — which accepted spontaneously that Bush was now waging a legitimate "war on terrorism." Domestic opinion was galvanised for a struggle comparable to the Cold War itself, providing Bush and his entourage with an opportunity to recast the terms of American global strategy more decisively than would otherwise have been possible.

The new "national security strategy" of the Bush administration, released to the public on September 20, 2002, expanded the rationale for using "pre-emptive" strikes.

Washington declared its intention of maintaining an immense military and economic edge over any competitor or would-be competitor. It sanctioned positioning the US military machine far more aggressively around the world, because America was now "menaced less by fleets and armies than by catastrophic technologies in the hands of an embittered few." [5] In a widely reported speech to an audience in Michigan, Bush declared: "We need to think about Saddam Hussein using Al Qaeda to do his dirty work." The US was compelled to "pursue the enemy before they hurt us again". This imprecation had been endlessly repeated by vast sections of the media by the time a former FBI translator with top-security clearance told the London *Independent* newspaper on March 2, 2004 that senior US officials had detailed information that Islamic terrorists were likely to attack the US with aircraft months before the attacks happened. The translator, Sibel Edmonds, described as "an outrageous lie" the claim by the national security adviser Rice that there was no such information.[6]

Edmonds's charge came as the White House was trying to fend off former US counter-terrorism chief Richard Clarke's testimony to the National Commission on Terrorist Attacks Upon the United States that the administration did not take serious measures to combat the threat of Islamic terrorism against the US in the months leading up to September 11. Clarke was the White House's national co-ordinator for security and counter-terrorism on the president's National Security Council for more than eight years. During that time he worked inside the White House for former presidents George HW Bush, Bill Clinton, and, of course, George W Bush. Just one week prior to the September 11 attacks, Clarke had sent a letter to security adviser Rice, criticising policymakers, the CIA, and the Pentagon for failing to adopt effective counter-measures against the threat of an attack on the US by radical Islamists. Embarrassingly for the Bush administration, Clarke's testimony at the congressional inquiry coincided with publication of his book *Against All Enemies*, which was scathing about the administration's failure to prevent the September 11 attacks. The book also confirmed just how dishonestly Bush's administration had behaved both before and after the attacks. According to Clarke, on the morning after 9/11, defence secretary Donald Rumsfeld suggested attacking Iraq in the total absence of any evidence linking Saddam Hussein's regime to the attack on New York City and the Pentagon.

In Clarke's view, the Bush administration was intent on using September 11 as an excuse to attack Iraq as part of a previously set political agenda. In short, Bush and his inner circle had a predetermined objective to attack and conquer Iraq, and then attempted to use the events of September 11 as justification to proceed toward that objective. As Clarke describes it: "... while the World Trade Centre was still smouldering, while they were still digging bodies out, people at the White House were thinking, 'This gives us the opportunity we've been looking for to go after Iraq'."[7]

According to Bush's own former treasury secretary, Paul O'Neil, the coming war with Iraq was discussed even before that — within days of the Bush administration's arrival in the White House. "It was all about finding a way to do it. That was the tone of it. The president saying, 'Go find me a way to do this'", O'Neil told CBS News on September. 4, 2002: "Barely five hours after American Airlines Flight 77 plowed into the Pentagon, Defence Secretary Donald Rumsfeld was telling his aides to come up with plans for striking Iraq, even though there was no evidence linking Saddam Hussein to the attacks." Congress then voted obligingly for an unnecessary war in order to pursue an undeclared policy that legislators did not fully understand, much less properly debate. The scene was set for British and American forces to invade a nation already devastated by two earlier wars and by 10 years of economic sanctions, and surrounded by enemies far better armed. Nevertheless, Iraq was "an imminent threat to world peace", and this would not be an invasion but a "pre-emptive action conducted in the humanitarian interests of the Iraqi people".

The British intelligence services and British prime minister Tony Blair co-operated closely with Bush and his administration to make a case for war while holding themselves aloof from awkward questions in public. In particular, they avoided explaining why US Secretary of State Colin Powell was provided with an allegedly confidential official British intelligence report on Iraqi "weapons of mass destruction" that was cited by Powell at the UN — and later turned out to have been plagiarised from open and unverified sources on the internet. A widely reported British and American intelligence operation to spy on UN Secretary General Kofi Annan and members of the UN Security Council was also glossed over by Blair and Bush. Nor did this encourage the UN to approve the invasion of Iraq.

Bush and his administration manipulated public opinion, and took the country into an illegal war with a rationale that defied common sense. Congress and influential sections of the media, by going along, were accessories to the fact. They impeded any committed effort to consider the full background to the events of September 11 and the full circumstances surrounding the decision to invade Iraq.

Certainly, no one in Congress or in the mainstream media was prepared to publish what Osama bin Laden himself had to say. In an audio tape recording transmitted via the internet in mid-April, 2004 at the height of the Congressional hearings, bin Laden informed Bush and the American public: "Labelling us and our acts as terrorism is also a description of you and of your acts. Reaction comes at the same level as the original action. Our acts are reaction to your own acts, which are represented by the destruction and killing of our kinfolk in Afghanistan, Iraq and Palestine. Which religion considers your killed ones innocent and our killed ones worthless? And which principle considers your blood real blood and our blood water? Reciprocal treatment is fair and the one who starts injustice bears greater blame."

Congress's preliminary report on the terror attacks was notable also for withholding 28 pages dealing with Saudi involvement in terrorist funding. Serious questions remain as to why members of the Saudi Royal family with close business connections to the Bush family, were whisked out of the US at the behest of the White House immediately after September 11 without any kind of questioning. There were other omissions as well, in particular Washington's tangled involvements in the Middle East and with the House of Sa'ud, which had helped bring to full force a militant Islamic backlash against the West.

Former CIA "foot soldier" Robert Baer, in his memoir *Sleeping With the Devil* describes a pervasive symbiosis between Saudi Arabia and the US, based on America's addiction to cheap oil and the spending in America of Saudi petrodollars.[8] The Saudi Royal family, with business links to the White House, is described by Baer as utterly corrupt, squandering their country's vast oil reserves on vanity projects, partying, gambling, sexual escapades, and the like. The Royal family's excesses ensure that the disaffected Saudi masses remain poor, uneducated, and in some quarters, rebellious. To distract the domestic masses from the royal family's excesses, according to Baer, it buys off Muslim extremists by funding Islamic charities and projects, especially the Muslim *madrasah* schools that are the breeding ground of anti-western sentiment and future Islamic terrorists. Baer describes a deeply entrenched pattern whereby the Saudi Royal family substitutes graft for governance and payoffs for political reforms, including large donations that have unintentionally ended up in the coffers of radical Islamist networks such as "al-Qaeda".

Given the precarious state of the Saudi Royal House and the potential threat that instability poses to important US military bases in the country, it is not surprising that the Bush administration felt a sense of urgency in setting up alternative, permanent bases in Iraq. There were also potentially catastrophic consequences for Western economies should the "wrong" elements gain control of Saudi oil reserves, hence America's need to secure Iraq's reserves, the second largest proven reserves in the world, as an insurance policy against Saudi instability.

Most of the 20 hijackers identified as having been involved in the September 11 massacre proved to be Saudi citizens — not Afghanis, as mistakenly believed by most Americans and misreported by sections of the media. Nor had the hijackers been recruited in Afghanistan. Most of the hijackers, and the plot leader Mohammed Atta, met while students in Hamburg, Germany. Another hijacker, Zacarias Moussaoui, was a French-born Muslim who fell in with fundamentalists at a mosque in London; and Khalid Sheikh Mohammed, one of the key planners of the September 11 attacks, studied at university in North Carolina.[9] This kind of information has often been passed over, perhaps because it raises uncomfortable questions for Washington, and makes it more difficult to invade foreign countries like Afghanistan and Iraq, and bomb their people to smithereens for "harbouring terrorists".

Similarly overlooked is the West's role in allowing the movement of Islamic militants in the early to mid-1990s, from the Middle East and Central Asia into Europe. Western intervention in Afghanistan may have created the *mujahidin*, but Western intervention in the Balkans succeeded in globalising it. In the early 1990s, with Western backing, many *mujahidin* moved from Afghanistan to fight on the Muslim side in Bosnia. Some had been trained by the CIA in Pakistan From 1992 onwards, the US also permitted the movement of up to 4,000 *mujahidin* volunteers from other parts of the Middle East, and from Central Asia and North Africa, to fight alongside Muslims in Bosnia against the Serbian and Croatian nationalists. Starting in 1992 from the Middle East, Central Asia and North Africa they moved to Bosnia to fight Serbian and Croatian nationalists on behalf of Bosnian Muslims.[10]

By the end of the 1990s, US officials were belatedly concerned about the *mujahidin* presence in the Balkans. In 2000, the US State Department under the Clinton administration finally prepared a report claiming that "hundreds of foreign Islamic extremists who became Bosnian citizens after battling Serbian and Croatian forces present a potential terrorist threat to Europe and the United States."[11] One year before the 11 September attacks, the State Department was worried that "the extremists [in Bosnia] include hardcore terrorists, some with ties to bin Laden", and that Bosnia-Herzegovina had become a "staging area and safe haven for terrorists"[12]. Clinton officials eventually appealed to the Sarajevo government to expel the *mujahidin*. But it was too late.

From Afghanistan at the close of the Cold War through to the Balkans in the "humanitarian" era, it was Western intervention and traditional public indifference to foreign conflicts that created the conditions in which Islamic terrorism would flourish. Initial US support for the *mujahidin* in Bosnia turned a specifically Central Asian issue — in which Muslim volunteers from various countries arrived in Afghanistan to take on the Red Army — into something much broader: a globalised phenomenon that was to haunt Americans at home and their allies abroad.

Chapter 12:

Profits of Doom

On March 23, 2003 the US Army's 507th Maintenance Company was ambushed by Iraqi troops in Iraq's southern city of Nasiriyah. Among the group of 10 American soldiers captured by the Iraqis was a Private Jessica Lynch. She was, according to the approved version of events, captured after firing at the Iraqis until her ammunition ran out, had been hit by a bullet, stabbed, tied up, and taken to a hospital in Nasiriyah where she was beaten repeatedly by an Iraqi officer. A week later, the official story goes, US special forces freed her in a surprise operation: despite stiff resistance from her guards, the US forces broke into the hospital, rescued her at great risk to themselves and flew her by helicopter to Kuwait.

Predictably, the media splashed the story, and the saving of Private Lynch came to represent the most heroic moment — perhaps the only heroic moment — of the war in Iraq. Twenty-year old Private Lynch had joined the army to get an education and become a kindergarten teacher. Instead, her rescue on April 1 turned her into an overnight media celebrity when, from the White House, President Bush announced her rescue to the nation. Eight days later the Pentagon supplied the world's media with a video made during the rescue mission, with scenes reminiscent of the best Hollywood war-action movies ever made.

On April 9, after the invasion of Iraq was complete, journalists from *The New York Times*, the *Toronto Star*, *El País* and the BBC went to Nasiriyah to expand the Lynch rescue story.

They were surprised by what they found. According to their interviews with Iraqi doctors who had looked after Lynch — and confirmed by US doctors who had later examined her — her wounds, a fractured arm and leg and a dislocated ankle, were not due to bullets but to the crash of a lorry in which she was travelling. She had not been maltreated. On the contrary, the Iraqi doctors had done everything possible to look after her, and had in fact saved her life by giving her blood transfusions. At considerable risk to themselves, these doctors managed to contact the US army to arrange the return of the injured soldier. Just two days before the special forces burst into the hospital, the doctors had even taken Lynch in an ambulance to a location close to the US lines, where US soldiers opened fire and almost killed her.[1]

The pre-dawn arrival of special forces equipped with sophisticated equipment astonished the Iraqi hospital staff. The doctors had already told the US forces that the Iraqi army had retreated, and that Lynch was waiting to be claimed. Dr Anmar Uday told the BBC's John Kampfner: "It was like in a Hollywood film. There were no Iraqi soldiers, but the American special forces were firing their weapons. They fired at random and we heard explosions. They were shouting Go! Go! Go! The attack on the hospital was a kind of show, or an action film with Sylvester Stallone".[2]

The "rescue" was filmed on a night-vision camera by a former assistant of director Ridley Scott, who had two years earlier worked on the Hollywood action movie *Black Hawk Down*. According to Robert Scheer of the *Los Angeles Times*, these images were then sent for editing to US central command in Qatar, and once they had been checked by the Pentagon they were distributed around the world.[3] It was one for the annals of propaganda, but not the first and certainly not the last.

On February 20, 2002 the *New York Times* had already revealed that the Pentagon, on orders from defence secretary

Donald Rumsfeld and defence under-secretary Douglas Feith, had secretly created a mysterious Office of Strategic Influence (OSI), to generate false news to serve US interests. It was co-ordinated by General Simon Worden. The OSI was authorised to engage in subversive propaganda, particularly to foreign media. It had a contract worth $100,000 a month with the Rendon Group, a media consultancy already used in the first Gulf war, which had fabricated a statement by a Kuwaiti "nurse" who claimed to have seen Iraqi soldiers looting the maternity department of a hospital in Kuwait and "killing the babies". The media splashed the story, and the "nurse's" statement was decisive in persuading members of Congress to vote for the war. Only later did it emerge that this "nurse" was in fact the daughter of the Kuwaiti ambassador in Washington, and her story was created for the Rendon Group consultancy by Michael K Deaver, formerly media adviser to Ronald Reagan.

In the run-up to the invasion, before critical votes in Congress and the United Nations on going to war in Iraq, senior administration officials, including Bush, had expressed certainty in public that Iraq possessed chemical and biological weapons. This was at a time when US intelligence agencies themselves were reporting they had no direct evidence that such weapons existed. According to Vincent Cannistrano, former head of CIA counter-intelligence, "cooked information" was working its way into high-level pronouncements.[4] Secretary of Defence Donald Rumsfeld created a Pentagon operation "to search for information on Iraq's hostile intentions or links to terrorists" — despite CIA reports saying there were none. Douglas Feith, the Undersecretary of Defense for Policy, acknowledged that he created a small intelligence team inside his office shortly after the attacks on September 11, 2001, to search for terrorist links with Iraq and other countries that he suggested the nation's spy agencies may have overlooked. Among the team's most prominent findings were suspected linkages between Iraq and al-

Qaeda, a conclusion doubted by the CIA and the Defence Intelligence Agency.[5]

While Feith's team at the Pentagon invented pretexts for war, Vice President Cheney personally went to the CIA headquarters in Langley, in a series of highly unusual visits. As the *Washington Post* disclosed on June 6, 2003: "Multiple visits to the CIA by Vice-President Dick Cheney created an environment in which some analysts felt they were being pressured to make their assessments on Iraq fit with Bush administration policy objectives, intelligence officials said ... The visits `sent signals, intended or otherwise, that a certain output was desired from here,' one agency official said."

For the benefit of the media, a certain output was certainly provided by a US-funded Iraqi exile group calling itself the Iraqi National Congress (INC), led by Ahmad Chalabi, a convicted embezzler who had been living in the West for the past 45 years.[*] It was Chalabi who had provided "crucial intelligence" on Iraqi weaponry to justify the invasion, almost all of which turned out to be false. He also laid out a rosy scenario about the readiness of the Iraqi people to welcome the invading forces as "liberators".

The INC's so-called Information Collection Programme — financed out of the more than $18 million that Congress approved for the group — also fed disinformation to mainstream newspapers, news agencies and magazines in the US, Britain and Australia. The articles had an effect of reinforcing Bush's claims that Saddam must be ousted because he was in league with

---

* In 1992 a Jordanian court convicted Chalabi in his absence of embezzling millions from Petra Bank whose 1989 collapse shook Jordan's political and financial system, forcing it to spend in excess of $400 million to bail out depositors. A sentence of 22 years hard labour awaits Chalabi if he ever sets foot again in Jordan. Chalabi returned to postwar Iraq in April 2003 as a member of the US's so-called Iraqi Governing Council. The INC reportedly remained on the Pentagon's payroll until at least 2004.

Osama bin Laden, was developing nuclear weapons, and was hiding biological and chemical weapons. These allegations, coming from a handful of self-styled Iraqi defectors, were not corroborated by other intelligence, and were hotly disputed by intelligence professionals at the CIA, the Defence Department and the State Department. The INC information conveniently bypassed official US intelligence channels and reached the recipients even after CIA, Defense Intelligence Agency and FBI officers started questioning the accuracy of the materials or the motives of those who supplied them. Nevertheless, information fed by the INC to the news media, as well as to selected administration officials and members of Congress, helped foster an impression that there were multiple sources of intelligence on Iraq's illicit weapons programs and links to bin Laden.[6]

The New York Times, quoting an unnamed Iraqi lieutenant-general supposedly linked to INC, published an article on November 8, 2001, to the effect that Iraq was hosting a secret training camp in the country, where terrorists were taught how to hijack airliners. In a November 11 article appearing in the London *Observer* the same source was quoted as saying that "the method used on 11 September perfectly coincides with the training I saw at the camp." The INC also alleged Iraq could launch toxin-armed Scud missiles at Israel that could kill 100,000 people and was aggressively developing nuclear weapons.

Articles originated by the INC appeared in *The New York Times* and the London *Observer*, but also in *The Washington Post*, *Vanity Fair*, *The Atlantic Monthly*, *The Times* of London, *The Sunday Times* of London, *The Sunday Age* of Melbourne in Australia, *The Kansas City Star* and *The Philadelphia Daily News*. The Associated Press and others similarly wrote stories based on INC-provided materials.[7]

The claims also found their way into official administration statements. US officials and others who supported a pre-emptive invasion quoted the allegations without anyone running the risk of contravening restrictions on classified information, or raising doubts about the defectors' reliability — even though many of the articles had noted that the information they contained could not be independently verified.[8] By mid-January 2002, polls showed that a solid majority of Americans favoured military force to oust Saddam.

In at least one case, the INC made a defector available to a journalist before his information had even been reviewed by official intelligence analysts. The defector, an engineer named Adnan Ihsan al Haideri, was interviewed by *New York Times* reporter Judith Miller, whose shrill, scare-mongering articles about Saddam and his alleged weapons of mass destruction probably did more than any other US journalist to influence pro-war opinion. She reported in a December 20, 2001 article in *New York Times* that there were biological, nuclear and chemical warfare facilities under private villas, the Saddam Hussein Hospital and fake water wells around Baghdad. On-site searches by UN weapons inspectors failed subsequently to discover any evidence to support the claims.[*]

Miller published numerous other articles for the *New York Times*, claiming that Saddam was developing chemical, biological and nuclear weapons. One such item was entitled "CIA hunts Iraq tie to Soviet smallpox", published in the *New York Times* on December 3, 2002. Miller wrote: "The CIA is investigating an informant's accusation that Iraq obtained a

---

* Miller and two other *New York Times* journalists had co-authored a book, *Germs: The Ultimate Weapon* published in October 2001, about the alleged proliferation of chemical and biological weapons in the hands of terrorist groups and "rogue states" following the demise of the Soviet Union. It fed off the 11 September attacks for its publication success in late 2001, making it one of the earliest publications to draw a dubious link between Iraq's alleged chemical weapons programme and the possibility of further terrorist attacks in the West. The book jacket proudly quotes one critic: "Deeply scary... Alarming... tragically important book.'" (Judith Miller, Stephen Engelberg, William Broad, *Germs: The Ultimate Weapon*, New York: Simon and Schuster, 2001).

particularly virulent strain of smallpox from a Russian scientist who worked in a smallpox lab in Moscow during Soviet times." Her articles were notable for their prolific use of unnamed sources such as "senior American officials", "foreign scientists", and an "informant whose identity cannot be disclosed". In May 2003, it was revealed that the main anonymous Iraqi source for most of her "front-page exclusives", was none other than INC leader Ahmad Chalabi.[9]

International experts on weapons, meanwhile, had been arguing long before the invasion started that official US accusations were false. According to senior UN weapons inspector, Scott Ritter: "Under the most stringent on-site inspection regime in the history of arms control ... No evidence of anthrax or any other biological agent was discovered."[10]

These inspections had been conducted thoroughly in terms of United Nations Resolution 687, declaring that Iraq must "unconditionally accept" the "destruction, removal or rendering harmless of its weapons of mass destruction." The resolution was passed by the UN in 1991 shortly after Iraq's defeat in the first Gulf War, which had stopped just short of actually removing Saddam from power due to fear of completely destabilising the region.

A decade later, the Bush administration had no such qualms. It sought to justify a "preventive war" that the UN and global opinion did not want. Some 1,500 American investigators of the UN's Iraq Survey Group had scoured the Iraqi countryside for evidence of weapons of mass destruction that they did not find. They also searched for documents that would have enabled them to assemble a clear, if somewhat circumstantial, case that Iraq had or intended to produce prohibited weapons. None were found. Yet unsubstantiated allegations of Iraq's chemical and biological weapons and its alleged nuclear capability continued to serve as an ostensible *casus belli* to appeal to the UN and recruit a few trigger-happy accomplices such as the United Kingdom and

Spain to Bush's project for the conquest of Iraq. It seems unlikely, to say the least, that Bush would have given the order for his troops to invade Iraq had there in fact been any risk at all of exposure to chemical and biological weapons.

Still, the dossier against Saddam that President George Bush presented to the UN General Assembly on September 12, 2002 claimed that Iraq was a threat to the security of the US because it had "weapons of mass destruction" — a catchy phrase first used by the Soviet Union during the Cold War, in reference to the US's own military arsenal. The claim was made at a time when Bush had already received reports from his security services proving his claims to be false.[11] On 24 September 2002, British Prime Minister Tony Blair contributed to the scare-mongering when he announced to the British House of Commons: "Iraq possesses chemical and biological weapons ... Its missiles can be deployed in 45 minutes." On February 5, 2003 the UN Security Council was assured by the US representative: "Saddam Hussein has investigated dozens of biological agents causing diseases such as gas gangrene, plague, typhus, tetanus, cholera, camelpox and haemorrhagic fever."

A secret department at the heart of the Pentagon played a significant part in generating such lies. An Office of Special Plans (OSP) was set up by Paul Wolfowitz, number two at the Defence Department, who later admitted that lies had been told. The decision to put forward the threat of weapons of mass destruction to justify a preventive war against Iraq, Wolfowitz confessed, had been adopted "for reasons that have a lot to do with US government bureaucracy ... We settled on the one issue which everyone could agree on, which was weapons of mass destruction".[12] That this consensus had been achieved on the basis of a scandalous deception was apparently beside the point.

According to former Lieutenant Colonel Karen Kwiatkowski, radical right-wingers of the Bush administration, including her superiors in the Pentagon planning department, bulldozed internal dissent, overlooked its own intelligence and relentlessly pushed for confrontation with Iraq. She resigned from the US military when she realised what was going on. Kwiatkowski, who was a political-military desk officer at the OSP, disclosed that the operations of OSP bypassed normal processes of accountability, developed subversive propaganda lines which were fed throughout government and to Congress, and even internally to the Pentagon, to make a misleading case for the immediate invasion of Iraq. It was in effect an intelligence operation to act as counter to the CIA, which was not coming up with any convincing evidence upon which to launch the invasion.[13] As Vincent Cannistrano, former head of CIA counter-intelligence told the *Guardian* on October 9, 2002: "Basically, cooked information is working its way into high-level pronouncements."

Middle East expert General Tony Zinn, the combatant commander of Central Command, was referred to as "a traitor" at an OSP staff meeting and removed by Bush when he spoke out publicly about some of the things that were being done at OSP. The presence or absence of weapons of mass destruction were never even debated by OSP members. To them, Saddam Hussein had to go, one way or another, and the decision to remove him was made fully a year before the invasion was launched. The ostensible search for weapons of mass destruction in Iraq, according to Kwiatkowski, was "a total whitewash effort. They didn't find anything, they didn't expect to find anything ... The truth is, we knew [Saddam] didn't have these things ... A pre-emptive war was based on what we knew was not a pressing need."[14]

On the eve of invasion, the US vice-president Dick Cheney announced: "We believe [Saddam] has reconstituted nuclear weapons."[15] Bush repeated the charges in many speeches and later embellished the charges with a few more lies: Iraq had sent bomb-making and document forgery experts to work with terrorist networks and had also provided them with chemical and biological weapons training, and so on. These charges were amplified by the pro-war media and repeated by television channels Fox News, CNN and MSNC, by the Clear Channel radio network via 1,225 stations throughout the US, and by newspapers such as the *Washington Post* and the *Wall Street Journal.* These accusations in turn provided the main argument for those who were pro-war around the world, including Bush's most sycophantic allies. "The Iraqi regime and its weapons of mass destruction represent a clear threat to world security", they declared in a declaration of support for the US on January 30 — the so-called "Letter of Eight", signed by among others Italy and Spain.[16]

A year later, on January 18, 2004 former chief UN arms inspector Dr Hans Blix told BBC radio news that the war on Iraq was not justified and that Washington and London had "over-interpreted" intelligence data, and that Iraq had not possessed weapons of mass destruction for at least 10 years before the war. A few days later, on January 23, American scientist Dr David Kay resigned as head of the US's Iraq Survey Group — a small army of 1,400 weapons experts who had thoroughly searched occupied Iraq for biological, chemical and nuclear weapons, and found none. He told National Public Radio: "We were almost all wrong, and I certainly include myself here." There were no nuclear, biological or chemical weapons of any kind. No stock-piles. No facilities for producing them. No hidden SCUD missiles, or other means of launching them. No research labs developing prototypes. Not a functioning gas shell. Not an ounce of uranium. Not an incriminating document. Nothing.

In the meantime, despite their public concern about the potentially destructive effects of banned weapons in Iraq, Bush, Blair and others somehow managed to overlook a malady that goes by the name of "Gulf War Syndrome". It is a potentially lethal medical disorder that first appeared among combat veterans of the 1990-1991 Gulf War. The most likely cause of the syndrome, according to experts, is the toxic side effects of depleted uranium ammunition (DU) used widely by the invading forces in Iraq. This is why, in 1996 a United Nations resolution classified DU ammunition as an illegal weapon of mass destruction. DU, or Uranium-238, is a waste product of power-generating nuclear reactors. It is used in armour piercing projectiles such tank shells and cruise missiles because it is 1.7 times denser than lead and burns as it flies. It also breaks up and vaporises after impact — which makes it potentially very deadly.

In 1991 alone, US forces fired 944,000 DU rounds in Kuwait and Iraq, each shell containing ten pounds of DU — not very radioactive individually but widely suspected of being capable in quantity of causing serious illnesses, blood abnormalities, and genetically transferred birth defects. One study of Gulf War veterans showed that their children had a higher possibility of being born with severe deformities, including missing eyes, blood infections, respiratory problems, and fused fingers.[17]

Dr Doug Rokke, a former Army colonel and professor of environmental science at Jacksonville University, was in charge of the military's environmental clean-up following the first Gulf War. When he criticised NATO commanders for not adequately protecting their troops in areas where DU ammunition was used, the Pentagon promptly sacked him. Just as the effects of Agent Orange during the Vietnam War were first explained away by the Pentagon as "post-traumatic stress disorder," "combat fatigue," or "shell shock," so the US deliberately played down the effects of DU weapons used in the first Gulf war and in US actions against Serbian forces in Kosovo in 1999. Because the military relied more heavily on DU munitions in the second Iraq War than in the first, post-war casualties may be even greater. According to the sacked Dr Rokke, between August 1990 and May 2002, even before the second Gulf war, a total of 262,586 soldiers became categorised as "disabled veterans" and 10,617 have died. His numbers, corroborated in part by the Veterans Administration, produce a US casualty rate for the whole decade of 30.8% — which is very much higher than the official Pentagon figures. [18] The Iraqi military and civilian casualty figures resulting from the American's use of DU weapons are probably incalculable. But never mind, banned weapons are perfectly acceptable — just as long as no one else uses them, and certainly not the Iraqis. Not even notionally.*

As for Iraqi documentation that probably could have proved or disproved British and American claims that Saddam possessed banned weapons, these were housed in the archives of Iraq's National Monitoring Directorate, the government agency responsible for co-ordinating all aspects of the United Nations weapons inspection programme. The directorate was also

---

* There is a long tradition of lies and hypocrisy surrounding banned weapons. Both Britain and the United States have themselves been unwilling to destroy their own stocks of bacteriological, biological and bio-chemical toxin weapons. In 1969 the two countries collaborated successfully on the transfer of genes between different strains of plague bacillus at the British Army's Porton Down Biological Warfare Laboratory and the US Army's Biological Warfare Laboratory at Fort Detrick in Frederick, Maryland. Britain and America, despite having ratified the 1972 Geneva Protocol banning biological and bacteriological weapons, continued biological warfare research for "defensive purposes only" — a distinction rendered meaningless by the fact there is no difference between offensive and defensive biological warfare research. Studies aimed at protection against biological attack, as the Stockholm International Peace Research Institute pointed out in 1983, are indistinguishable from those necessary to prepare micro-organisms for attack. [Charles Piller, "DNA -- Key to Biological Warfare?", *The Nation*, 10-18 December 1983, p.598, quoting study by Stockholm International Peace Research Institute]. Not only did the US continue its research in biological warfare for "defensive purposes" but it conferred respectability on its biological warfare facility at Fort Detrick by misleadingly renaming it the US Army Medical Research Institute for Infectious Disease. Its staff and budget were trebled within two years of America having ratified the Geneva Protocol. [Robert Harris and Jeremy Paxman, *A Higher Form of Killing*, New York: Hill and Wange, 1982, p.266].

responsible for monitoring Iraq's industrial infrastructure and ensuring compliance with UN Security Council resolutions regarding disarmament, verification and export-import controls. As such, the directorate was the repository for every Iraqi government record relating to its weapons programmes, as well as to the activities at dozens of industrial sites in Iraq that were "dual-use" — used to manufacture permitted items but capable of being modified to manufacture proscribed material. A 12,500 page "full, final and complete declaration" provided by Iraq to the United Nations in 2002 was compiled using this archive. Every interview conducted by the United Nations inspectors with Iraqi scientists throughout the 1990s was videotaped and available for review at the directorate, as evidence that Iraq was complying with the UN resolutions — something that was not proved false after the American-led invasion.

The entire archive had been consolidated into metal containers before the invasion and stored at the directorate's Jadariyah headquarters for protection. On April 8 the building was occupied by units from the Army's Third Infantry Division. No-one from the US intelligence services or from the coalition high command showed up or expressed any interest in taking control of the archive. Rather, after occupying the facility for two weeks, the American soldiers simply withdrew, allowing looters to ransack the facility completely, destroy its records and steal every computer in sight.[19]

George W Bush, meanwhile, continued to warn the American public and the world at large: "A new totalitarian threat has risen against civilisation". His warning was not meant to be taken as self-referential, nor as a reference to corporate America, which was raking in the dollars. The US-led Coalition Provisional Authority had ordered the dismantling of fundamental elements of Iraq's moderately socialist economy and instituted wide-ranging capitalist reforms. International corporations were invited to bid for full foreign ownership in just about every sector of the Iraqi economy. Singled out for special attention in the privatisation of Iraq were plans to dismantle anything that smacked of socialism — in particular Saddam's food distribution system, once described by the UN as the world's most efficient food network, but now viewed by the American administrator of Iraq as "a dangerous anachronism".[20]

In the ruins of Iraq, US companies with intimate ties to the White House, such as Kellogg, Brown & Root (KBR), a subsidiary of Halliburton Corporation, US Vice President Dick Cheney's former firm, were set to make a fortune in the aftermath of the illegal, US-led invasion. By September 2003, KBR had billed the US government about $950 million for work completed under an exclusive contract capped at $8.2 billion to rebuild Iraq's oil infrastructure.[21] By mid-2004, and with troop commitments growing, congressional researchers and independent economists were predicting that the cost of Halliburton's contract alone could top $150 billion through the next fiscal year — as much as three times what the White House had originally estimated, and the war and continuing occupation could total $300 billion over the next decade.[*]

Oil and money were central features of the war on Iraq in other ways as well. It is reasonable to conjecture that the true reason for the invasion was the currency switch Saddam had made in November 2000 in the Food for Oil programme, from the dollar to the euro. The dollar's dominance of the international oil trade had originally been cemented in the immediate post-World War II years, when the Bretton Woods Conference established the dollar as the world standard virtually replacing gold. This allowed the US to run huge budget deficits in both

---

[*] *Time* magazine reported on June 7, 2004 it had obtained an internal Pentagon e-mail dated March 5, 2003, sent by an Army Corps of Engineers official confirming "action" on the granting of a multibillion-dollar Halliburton contract to restore Iraqi oil supplies was "coordinated" by Cheney's office, without other bids being sought.

domestic expenditure and international trade.

While the US prints dollars to meet its fiscal obligations, most countries around the world accept dollar payments for their goods because of the dollar's value as the currency of choice for oil purchases. As a result, the US retains its economic dominance as the producer of the currency of oil trade, while less developed countries are forced into a cycle of dependence on America in order to buy oil. The demand for dollars as the universal oil currency, in turn, has allowed successive US administrations to commit enormous resources to defence production, making it the mightiest military power in history. In sum, Iraq was attacked neither because of its alleged links to al-Qaeda nor its possession of "weapons of mass destruction", but because it threatened the hegemony of the American dollar.

The decision to invade Iraq was taken at a time when the US dollar was in an extremely sensitive period, and America was a debtor nation — in fact the most indebted country in the world with domestic and international debt approaching 3.4 trillion dollars or $12,000 for each man, woman and child in America. A long term weakening of the dollar due to its slipping hold on the world oil trade would thus have serious consequences for American prosperity and also its capacity to finance its military expenditure through deficit financing. That is to say, the euro, both then as now, threatened America's economic power as well as its military power. In short: a crisis in American capitalism under the Bush presidency. [22]

The Bush II years denoted the longest decline in industrial employment since the Great Depression, with a near doubling of long-term unemployment. Jobless claims were touching 450,000 a week. A $5.6 trillion — again, trillion — federal budget surplus at the time of Bush's inauguration had now devolved to a $4 trillion deficit. Plus the stock market, for the first time sine the 1930s, was off by double digits for the entire length of the Bush II regime to date. Economic chaos, in any terms.[23] If or when UN sanctions were lifted, as they would inevitably have to be at some point, oil sales from the country with the world's second largest oil reserves would have to be paid in euros, now that Saddam had switched the dollar to the euro. Other oil producing countries, notably Iran and Venezuela, would probably follow suit — resulting in a glacial shift in market confidence in trading on the dollar. The US-led invasion of Iraq sent a clear message to such countries of what could happen to them if they similarly switched to trading oil in euros. Significantly, one of the first executive orders that Bush signed in May 2003, immediately after the invasion, switched trading on Iraq's oil back to the dollar.

It was US President Calvin Coolidge who in 1925 uttered the famous line: "The business of America is business." Nowadays, an even more repugnant truth is that the business of America is the business of war.

Chapter 13:

The Future: Right Here, Right Now

George W Bush and his inner circle were thinking of a premeditated attack on Iraq even before Bush took office in January 2001. They intended to take military control of the Gulf region whether or not Saddam Hussein was in power. While the unresolved conflict with Iraq over weapons inspections provided the most convenient justification for an attack, as far as Bush and his colleagues were concerned, "the need for a substantial American force presence in the Gulf transcends the issue of the regime of Saddam Hussein."[1]

This much is clear from a document calling for "a revolution in American military affairs", published fully two years before the September 11 "al-Qaeda" attacks.* The organisation that published the document, the so-named Project for the New American Century (PNAC), was founded by people who were later to hold key positions in the Bush administration, such as Dick Cheney (now vice- president), Donald Rumsfeld (defence secretary), Paul Wolfowitz (Rumsfeld's deputy), George W Bush's younger brother Jeb and Lewis Libby (Cheney's chief of staff) —

---

* Despite the later Bush administration's ostensible abhorrence for chemical and biological weapons, the PNAC document also campaigned for, among other things, the development of advanced forms of biological warfare that "can target specific genotypes (and) may transform biological warfare from the realm of terror to a politically useful tool." [*Rebuilding America's Defenses: Strategies, Forces And Resources For A New Century*, Washington: Project for the New American Century (PNAC). September 2000, p.60]

all of them vociferous supporters of "the war against terrorism". Other PNAC members exerting influence on US policy were the President of the Committee for the Liberation of Iraq, Randy Scheunemann, Republican Party leader Bruce Jackson, and current PNAC chairman William Kristol, conservative writer for the *Weekly Standard.*

The main significance of America obtaining its first secure military base in a dependable client state at the heart of the world's main energy reserves, is that it would provide Washington with a tremendous lever of world control. The US military machine itself runs to great extent on oil. But the US-led invasion and occupation of Iraq was not just about oil and petrodollars. It was to a great extent about geopolitical dominance — and not just geopolitical dominance, but also the military domination of space.

The PNAC had campaigned vigorously for "full spectrum dominance", in which "an essential element" would be control of space – defined as "the ability to assure access to space, freedom of operations within the space medium, and an ability to deny others the use of space".[2] A central feature of this would be the augmentation of the US Space Command with a new "Space Service" thereby escalating U.S. military preparedness "from the theatre level to the global level" in order to achieve world-wide dominance both militarily and commercially.[3] But building the space stations and the satellites for the weaponisation of space, the document noted, would be an extremely expensive undertaking. One projection had the first stage of it being about a trillion dollars.

So an enormous amount of money has to be shifted from the American taxpayers and other parts of the economy to the military and the space command. The document noted that such a project would probably proceed very slowly in the absence of "some catastrophic and catalysing event such as a new Pearl Harbor".[4]

Whatever the truth as to whether or not the US government itself caused, encouraged or deliberately allowed the heinous events of September 11 to occur, it is certainly the case that the attacks provided a "catastrophic and catalysing event". In the immediate aftermath of the attacks, just one year after *Rebuilding America's Defenses* was published, and while plans for the invasion of Iraq were gaining momentum, Congress overwhelmingly approved the Bush administration's revitalised "Star Wars" programme, which had floundered under the Clinton administration.

It is also true that the new US national security strategy announced by the White House on September 17, 2002 bore some striking resemblances to the earlier PNAC document that had advocated "a revolution in US military affairs". The Bush administration announced it was, among other things, abandoning an international effort to strengthen the UN's Biological Weapons Convention against Germ Warfare, advising allies that further discussions would have to be delayed for four years.[5] A month later, the UN Committee on Disarmament adopted a resolution that called for stronger measures to prevent the militarisation of space, recognising this to be "a grave danger for international peace and security," and another that reaffirmed the 1925 Geneva Protocol prohibiting the use of poisonous gases and bacteriological methods of warfare. Both passed unanimously, with only two abstentions: the US and Israel.

A few weeks later, the US Space Command released plans to go beyond US "control" of space for military purposes to "ownership," which is to be permanent, in accord with the National Security Strategy. Ownership of space was "key to our nation's military effectiveness," permitting "instant engagement anywhere in the world. A viable, prompt, global strike capability, whether nuclear or non-nuclear, will allow the US to rapidly strike high-payoff, difficult-to-defeat targets from stand-off ranges and produce the desired effect... [and] to provide war-fighting commanders the ability to rapidly deny, delay, deceive, disrupt, destroy, exploit and neutralise targets in hours/minutes rather than weeks/days even when US and allied forces have a limited forward presence," thus reducing the need for overseas military bases.[6]

Similar plans without historical parallel had been outlined in a May 2002 Pentagon planning document, partially leaked, which called for a strategy of "forward deterrence" in which missiles launched from space platforms would be able to carry out almost instant "unwarned attacks." No target on the planet or in space would be immune to American attack. The US could strike without warning whenever and wherever a threat was perceived, and it would be protected by missile defences. Hypersonic drones would monitor and disrupt targets while surveillance systems would provide the ability to track, record and analyse the movement of every vehicle in a foreign city. The world would be left at the mercy of US attack at will, without warning or credible justification.[7]

Until then, and in all corners of the globe from the Philippines to Uzbekistan and Okinawa, and all stops between, American armed forces are today occupying a global empire of US military bases for the purposes of "protecting civilisation" from whatever. Since World War II, the US has been at war with or has attacked, among other countries, Cuba, Cambodia, El Salvador, Guatemala, Grenada, Korea, Laos, Libya, Nicaragua, Panama, Somalia, Sudan, Vietnam, and the former Yugoslavia. It has conducted covert operations throughout Africa, Asia, and Latin America, has violated international law, subverted consensual opinion, rigged elections, engineered violent coups, armed and supported dictators, undermined democracies, backed Israel's war on Lebanon and against the Palestinians, and played a crucial role during the 1980s Afghan civil war in which more than one million people, mainly civilians, were killed. Add it all up, and the picture that emerges is of a veritable World War III, in which the US government is the chief protagonist and the US military-industrial complex the chief benefactor.

At a time when US arms sales dwarf those of its nearest competitor — Russia — by a ratio of more than 9-to-1, US defence contractors continue to receive billions of tax dollars in subsidies. This money is poured into the pockets of armaments manufacturers because they need to "remain competitive" around the globe. The US military-industrial complex continues to employ hundreds of thousands of people, raking in billions of dollars in profits every year, with a veritable army of lobbyists and Washington insiders to maintain its dominant position in the US economy. The US Federal budget currently stands without precedent at more than $343 billion for military expenditure including "humanitarian" crusades.[*]

No amount of military expenditure, however, might improve the morale of those who are actually doing the fighting in pursuit of America's hegemonic expansion. A survey published on October 16, 2003 by the US military newspaper *Stars and Stripes*, for example, found the morale of US soldiers in Iraq so low that half of them said they were unlikely to remain in the armed forces. Many complained their mission was "not clearly defined" or "not at all defined". They were wondering, after eight months in Iraq, what the war was for, whom it was against, whether or not they had won, what they were supposed to be doing now, what they might be expected to do next and what threat would be conjured up by the Bush administration to justify it. What the occupying force did know with certainty was that their casualties were increasing daily, no weapons of mass destruction had been found, and there had not been a specific incident or any real threat to justify a full-scale invasion. In short, they had been duped. Just like millions of others. By early May

---

[*] The same budget allocates a paltry $1 billion to help combat world hunger, the real threat to global security.

2004 the *Army Times* newspaper was demanding that top political leaders should be held accountable

The old French saying *C'est la guerre* — such is war — captures the notion that war is dirty and bloody, yet sometimes worth it. But that rings hollow today. For many US soldiers the very notion of a truth that is worth fighting and dying for has been called into question, and many have become increasingly uncomfortable with the idea of fighting and dying for a cause, whatever that cause is officially described to be. At the same time, public mistrust has become institutionalised, a habit. It is all around us. "Trust nobody" the T-shirts proclaim. Most people don't even care if public officials lie to them. Many seem to expect it. No wonder Western societies are coming apart at the seams. Trust is the bond that holds society together, and trust is based on truth. Not to be duped about the past is of vital importance to a society's future; and it is central to a healthy cultural identity.

This is why most people today find it difficult to believe in politics or in politicians, and many don't believe in anything much at all. People are disillusioned. This is not mere, healthy questioning of those in authority. It reflects a culture of fear and vulnerability, a destructive phenomenon of the age, based on cynicism and something akin to rampant paranoia — a sense that we are all powerless victims at the mercy of dark forces. Official lying, directly or indirectly, has eroded public trust and it has resulted in a loss of individual reference points. This poses a far greater threat to the health of the Western society of nations than any weapons of mass destruction ever supposedly hidden in some Third World country such as Iraq.

This collective state of mind has not come out of the blue. It has reinforced what were already dominant trends in the public mind long before the lies leading up to the invasion of Iraq. Each new revelation of deception or of political intrigue on the part of those in power has merely bolstered public cynicism.

"So what? They all do it", is a common response. Such large-scale mistrust of officialdom accumulated gradually and fragmentarily until the body of evidence became so large as to be difficult to ignore. So often during World War II and the Cold War did governments assert their right to lie, to manage the news and contrive to deceive the public, that their lies about Iraq's "weapons of mass destruction" were almost irrelevant.

The public mood is not just anti-politician, but anti-politics — an institutionalised mistrust that is corrosive of democracy and of public life. In the United States, about half the electorate — tens of million people — did not even bother to vote in the dubious election of 2000 which gained George W Bush his presidency. In Britain during 2001, Tony Blair's New Labour party achieved an election victory based on the lowest electoral turnout for decades. Since then, according to recent figures, membership of the major political parties in Britain has fallen by half since 1980. During the same period, political party membership in France has declined by two-thirds, and in Italy by 51 percent.[8]

One conclusion to be reached from all this is that a culture of cynicism, voter apathy and mistrust does not distinguish between good and bad governance — all government policy statements are treated as lies. It is taken for granted by vast sections of the public that governments will lie to us if they possibly can, and whether or not they actually do so does not even matter any more. It is a manifestation of the paradox that covert actions have public outcomes. We assume we are being lied to because, most of the time, we are actually being lied to. The present derives from the past and the future from both.

The October 2003 election of Arnold Schwarzenegger as governor of California, America's most populous state and the world's sixth largest economy, is indicative of the triumph of cynicism over politics. Schwarzenegger's candidacy became a focus of Californians, not because of any impressive political ideas on his part, but rather because he has none at all. He is the very antithesis of a politician. Some of his fans may have voted for Arnie the actor, but the rest of California voted for Arnie the buffoon — the perfect anti-politician. Nor is the present-day culture of political mistrust, cynicism and voter disillusionment an exclusively Anglo-American phenomenon. It can be discerned throughout the post-modern Western society of nations and spheres of influence. In newly democratic Serbia, for instance, the outcome of national elections was annulled on 15 November 2003, because insufficient numbers of voters turned out to cast their ballots. And in newly democratic South Africa 80% of young adults between the ages of 18 and 24 did not even bother to register as voters in that country's 2004 democratic elections

The universal decline of party membership coincides with a wider disengagement from political life. Today, most people's idealism and hopes are rarely invested in a belief in political change, and individuals rarely develop their identities through some form of socio-political attachment. The cultural effects of this can be recognised in a certain retreat from society into the safety of one's imagination as evidenced by the popularity of multiple Oscar-winning films such *Lord of the Rings*. It bespeaks an unhealthy preoccupation with otherworldly things, at the expense of being engaged with the real world inhabited by real people, and it is an example of what happens when people lose the will to confront reality. This is democracy's moment of truth: the moral certainties of the past have become seriously eroded, while no new moral consensus has emerged.

There has of course always been some degree of scepticism about politicians — but that was something quite different from today's automatic assumption that they are all liars and cheats. The moral high ground has been exchanged for a culture of cynicism and incipient paranoia. Western society has arrived from a worldview ordered around blind faith in "democratic" governance to a psycho-social phenomenon in which large numbers of people today experience some form of free-floating doubt and anxiety about everything. Collective institutions such as the United Nations and humanist projects of all kinds seem to have collapsed, leaving most people today without any resolve with which to respond decisively to events.

Public disenchantment with politics has bred outright scepticism about any attempt by the political elite to exercise anything even vaguely resembling integrity. People experience historic events as being beyond their control and they tend understandably to see real or imagined conspiracies behind everything. The perceived truth of any one conspiracy theory lends credence to all the others, eating away at whom we trust and what we believe in, and this provides more fuel for the mass escape to cynicism. The media, meanwhile, dutifully reinforces the depths of moral confusion that characterise contemporary times.

There is nothing positive about the spread of New Age angst and an anti-political mood that is based on apathy, disillusionment and knee-jerk cynicism. Its corrosive effects seep into our personal lives, inducing a philosophy of futility and focusing people on the banal and superficial things of life, such as unbridled acquisitiveness and the notion that "greed is good". Far from people being united, it is more a case of do nothing, say nothing — with everybody suspicious of the person next door. Clearly, if one can speak of a collective identity crisis, of a period of radical discontinuity in a people's sense of who and what they are, the present comes close to having attained that condition. Gone are the great public debates about moral values, social issues and our essential humanity. Cynicism has become woven into the very fabric of Western culture. And a cynic, as Oscar Wilde once observed, is "a person who knows the price of everything and the value of nothing".

Uncritical cynicism can only intensify notions of powerlessness rather than aid any meaningful transformation. If society values nothing and trusts nobody, then constructive social and political change is impossible. The cause of human progress and development becomes retarded because, among other things, it means unscrupulous political leaders can continue lying as they have always done in the past, but now without even bothering to hide it, regardless of how tattered their credibility becomes. The fallout from such a crisis of credibility is doing far more real damage to the legitimacy of democratic governance than any dirty little war in Iraq.

The passivity of the public and the willingness of most people to be spoon-fed the news without doing the work of engaging their minds also encourages many folk to indulge in an orgy of national self-righteousness about the "war on terrorism". They are blissfully unconcerned that other things might be afoot which may prove more important — such as the possibility their own government could have caused, encouraged or deliberately allowed such heinous events as the attacks of September 11 to occur. Nor do media owned by companies such as General Electric, which is one of the world's largest armaments manufacturers, tend to concern themselves with such matters. There is, for example, not even one reference in the US mainstream media archives to the petrodollar issue underlying the war on Iraq. What it effectively amounts to is a cartel of big corporations and government, in which the largest media conglomerates relieve government of the need for censorship by doing it themselves.

Yet "democracy" is meant to signify the main organiser of consensus as inferred from "consensual opinion". "Democracy" is also traditionally attached to the State, that is to the form of the State supposedly subscribed to in most political thinking. But this form of State inferred by consensual opinion has for more than half a century been subverted through an information stream heavily polluted by official lies, incitement, disinformation, deception and covert propaganda in all its forms.

Perhaps this is why profound changes are occurring beneath the surface of Western societies, principally in the form of a withering of the State. Although the word "democracy" derives from the Greek *demos* — the people — what we are experiencing today is not the will of the people in action, but the dissolution of any supposed opposition between dictatorship and democracy. Much as it voices the supposed interests and consensual opinions of social groups, democracy as a form of State is fast becoming *de facto* dissolved. It has finally succeeded in subverting its own legitimacy.

We are witnessing the end of statecraft, and the end of what was once the core of political life — the great debate over how best to create the Good Society. No amount of politically correct posturing can disguise the empty hole now at the heart of democracy. The dynamics between secrecy, governance, public opinion, and the media, and the replication in "peacetime" of wartime methods of news and information management, ensure that the "national interest" is subordinated to the needs of governance in maintaining control of the "national interest" as perceived by the public as a whole.

Hence, increasingly, the end of all relevance to the word "democracy". Governance has simply become a depoliticised, bureaucratic, managerial affair — politics as such having been reduced to mere personal parliamentary point scoring and a grim sifting by the political elite through each other's dirty washing.

Yet, there is no reason to believe that the process of human progress has come to an end, or that it ever will. There will always be people to stand up for decency and integrity, and to resist the filth of an age turned unheroic. Ordinary people may yet come to recognise the extent to which media commentary and analysis, and contemporary historical interpretation, catapult people into a safe moral universe of Good v Evil, uncomplicated by the moral dilemmas of the real world. It is a morally questionable world, into whose innermost fabric has become interwoven the longstanding Nazi propaganda dictum of "the bigger the lie, the better chance it has of succeeding."

Notes and References

Notes:

Introduction

1. John Lewis Gaddis, *Surprise, Security and the American Experience*, Cambridge MA: Harvard University Press, 2004, p.xii.

Prologue: 1898 - 1939

1. See L Snyder & R Morris (eds), *A Treasury of Great Reporting*, New York; Simon and Schuster, 1962, p.236.
2. This account draws on David Ramsay, *Lucitania, Saga and Myth*, New York: Norton, 2003; Diana Preston, *Lusitania: An Epic Tragedy*, New York: Walker, 2003; Cunard Archives http://www.liv.ac.uk/~archives/cunard/ships/lusitan.htm [Accessed 16 June 2003].
3. Preston, op cit, p.393.
4. Burton J Hendrick, *The Life and Times of Walter H Page* (1922), Chapter xiv, "The *Lusitania* – and after". Republished at http://www.liv.byu.edu/~rdh/wwi/memoir/Page/Page09htm
5. Hendrick, ibid.
6. Carroll Quigley, *Tragedy and Hope: A history of the world in our time*, New York: MacMillan, 1966.
7. Walter Lippmann, *Public Opinion*, London: Allen & Unwin, 1932, p.310. For further discussion see Noam Chomsky, *Towards a New Cold War*, New York: Pantheon, 1982, chapter 1. Also of interest is Edward S Herman & Noam Chomsky, *Manufacturing Consent*, New York: Pantheon, 1988.
8. See Edward Bernays, *Propaganda*, New York: HY Liveright, 1928.

9. Philip Knightley, *The First Casualty: The war correspondent as hero, propagandist and myth maker*, London: Quartet 1982, pp.66-67.

10. *The Bryce Report: Report of the Committee on Alleged German Outrages*, London: His Britannic Majesty's Government, 1915.

11. William Shirer, *The Rise and Fall of the Third Reich*, London: Pan 1965, pp.628-30, 719, 723; Paul W Blackstock, *The Strategy of Subversion: Manipulating the Politics of Other Nations*, Chicago: Quadrangle 1964, p.94.

12. Casualties estimated by Brookings Institution, Washington.

Part One: World War II, 1940-1943

Chapter 1: Manufacturing Hate

1. Winston Churchill, *The Great War*, 3 Vols, London: George Newnes, 1933, Vol.1, p.498.

2. FW Winterbotham, *The Ultra Secret*, London: Weidenfeld and Nicolson 1974, pp. 2-3.

3. Winterbotham, op cit, p.24: cf., FH Hinsley, *British Intelligence in the Second World War: Its influence on Strategy and Operations*, (4 vols), London: HMSO, 1977-1988 (official history); Ralph Bennett, *Ultra in the West*, London: Hutchinson 1979.

4. See official history, *Royal Air Force, 1939-1945*, 3 Vols, London: HMSO 1953-1954, Vol.1, p.210.

5. RV Jones interviewed by the author, September 1988.

6. Public Records Office (hereafter referred to as PRO) Air Ministry file AIR 2/5238, Air Staff memorandum to Prime Minister, 14 November 1940 -- Note for the Prime Minister on projected operation by German Air Force "Moonlight Sonata" and counter operation by the Metropolitan Air Force "Cold Water", para.6(c); Hinsley, op cit, Vol I, Appendix 9 - "Advance Intelligence: GAF Raid on Coventry: 14 Nov 1940."

7.   John Terraine, *A Time for Courage: The Royal Air Force in The European War 1939-1945*, New York: Macmillan 1985, p.266; Asher Lee, *Blitz on Britain*, London: Four-Square 1960, p.104; Hinsley, *British Intelligence in the Second World War*, Vol I, p.318.

8.   PRO AIR 2/5238, Air Staff memorandum to Prime Minister, 14 November 1940, para. 6(b).

9.   R Money-Kyrel, " The Psychology of Propaganda", *British Journal of Medical Psychology*, Vol 19, 1943.

10. PRO Information Ministry file INF 1/292 "Home Intelligence Weekly Report", 4-11 August 1942.

11. Winston Churchill, *The Second World War*, 6 Vols, London: Cassell, 1948-54, Vol.3, p.194.

12. MRD Foot, *SOE in France*, London: HMSO, 1966, p.12.

13. For the official version see *Royal Air Force* op cit, p.210; compare with: Cajus Bekker, *The Luftwaffe War Diaries*, London: Macdonald, 1966, p.164, Charles Webster & Noble Frankland, *The Strategic Air Offensive against Germany* (hereafter referred to as SAO), 4 Vols, London: HMSO, Vol 4, p.494; D Wood & D Dempster, *The Narrow Margin: the Battle of Britain and the Rise of Air Power 1930-1940*, London: Arrow, 1967, pp. 84, 477-8. In 1941 the numerical advantage in Britain's favour would rise to 49.5 percent.

14. John Masterman, *The Double Cross System*, London: Sphere 1973, p.79; Popov, Spy/Counterspy, London: Panther 1976, pp. 133, 171-73.

15. James Rusbridger & Eric Nave, *Betrayal at Pearl Harbor*, London: Michael O'Mara / New York: Simon & Schuster, 1991, pp. 25, 139. Nave's primary account is the only one known to have ever been published by anyone directly involved in Far East secret cryptographic operations during World War II.

16. Rusbridger & Nave, op cit, p. 140.

17. Robert Stinnert, *Day of Deceit*, New York: Free Press, 1999.

18. Stinnert, op cit, pp.291-2. Also of interest are: Lawrence S. Safford, "A Brief History of Communications Intelligence in the

United States", in Ronald H. Spector (ed.) *Listening to the Enemy: Key Documents on the Role of Communications Intelligence in the War with Japan*, Wilmington: Scholarly Resources 1988, p.10; Winterbotham, op cit, p.168; cf., *Report of the Joint Committee on the Investigation of the Pearl Harbor Attack*, Washington: Senate Document No.244, 79th Congress, "Recommendations", p.253.

19. Gordon W. Prange, *At Dawn We Slept*, Harmondsworth: Penguin 1981, p.402.

20. A Russell Buchanan (ed.), *The United States and World War II, Military and Diplomatic Documents*, "Pre-war Correspondence of German Diplomats in the United States", Columbia: University of South Carolina Press, 1972, pp.17-24.

21. Hemingway quoted in Cushing Strout, *The American Image of the Old World*, New York: Harper and Row, 1963, p.205.

22. Robert Jungk, *Brighter than 1000 Suns: A Personal History of the Atomic Scientists*, London: Gollancz and Hart-Davis, 1958, pp.108, 83-101; Richard Rhodes, *The Making of the Atomic Bomb*, Harmondsworth: Penguin 1988, pp.357, 372.

Chapter 2: Singapore

1.   JRM Butler, *History of the Second World War*. 4 Vols, London: HMSO, 1957, Vol 2 "Grand Strategy", pp.579, 581 (official history).

2.   S Woodburn Kirby, *Singapore: The Chain of Disaster*, London: Cassel 1971, p.140.

3.   Noel Barber, *Sinister Twilight: The Rise and Fall Again of Singapore*, London: Collins 1969, p.22.

4.   Barber, op cit, p.34.

5.   MRD Foot, *SOE: The Special Operations Executive 1940-1946*, London: BBC, 1984, pp.22-5

6.   Quoted in Barber, op cit, p.58.

7.   Barber, op cit, pp.37, 148.

8.   Barber, op cit, p.58.

9. Michael Howard, *British Intelligence in the Second World War: Strategic Deception*, (Official history), London: HMSO 1990, pp.xi-xii, 22, 32.

10. Kirby, op cit, pp.224ff, 25.

11. *Hansard*, House of Commons, 27 January 1941.

12. Winterbotham, op cit, p.168, and see Rusbridger & Nave, op cit, pp. 43, 55, 82, 93, 94, 96-98, 103, 104, 134-35. Also of interest are: David Kahn, "Codebreaking in World Wars I and II", *Historical Journal*, Vol 23 No 3 1980, pp.617-39; David Irving, *Churchill's War*, Vol I, "The Struggle for Power", Bullsbrook (Australia): Veritas, 1987, p.344.

13. Safford in Spector, op cit, p.10.

14. Kirby, op cit, p.225.

15. Information provided by Australian War Memorial, Canberra.

16. Yamashita quoted in Barber, op cit, pp.58, 156-7.

17. Quoted in Brian Montgomery, *Shenton of Singapore*, London: Leo Cooper/Secker and Warburg 1984, p.194.

18. Quoted in Kirby, op cit, pp.224-5, 252.

19. Information provided by Australian War Memorial, Australian Red Cross, and Association of Asian Studies, Ann Arbor, Michigan.

20. Information provided by departments of History and Asian studies at universities of Nanzan and Waseda, Japan.

21. See Mao Tse-tung, *Selected Works*, 4 Vols, Peking: Foreign Languages Press, 1967, Vol. 2, "Unite All Anti-Japanese Forces", pp. 389-94.

22. Montgomery, op cit, p.204.

23. For further discussion see Chapter 7 post. See also Association of Asian Studies, "Anti-Japanese Movements in Southeast Asia during World War II". Abstract (1996) www.aasianst.org/absts/1996abst/inter/i181.htm [Accessed 21 July 2003].

24. Of interest is Ian Trenowden, *Operations Most Secret: SOE, the Malayan Theatre*, London: Wm Kimber, 1978.

25. See Yoji Akashi, "MPAJA/Force 136 Resistance Against the

Japanese in Malaya, 1941-1945". Association of Asian Studies. Abstract (1996) www.aasianst.org/absts/1996abst/inter/ intertoc.htm [Accessed 21 July 2003].

26.   Christopher Thorne, *Allies of a Kind: The United States, Britain and the War against Japan, 1941-1945*, London: Hamish Hamilton, 1978, p.102.

27.   See: Spencer Chapman, *The Jungle is Neutral*, London: Chatto and Windus, 1948.

Chapter 3: Bomber Barons

1.   Directive cited in Norman Longmate, *The Bombers: The RAF Offensive Against Germany 1939-45*, London: Hutchinson, 1983, p.92.

2.   See Longmate, op cit, p.10 and cf., Alfred Price, *Instruments of Darkness: the History of Electronic Warfare*, London: Granada, 1979, p.109; Anthony Verrier, *The Bomber Offensive*, London: Batsford 1968, pp.326-9; Arthur William Tedder, *Air Power in War*, London: Hodder and Stoughton 1948, p.98;

3.   Charles Webster and Noble Frankland, *The Strategic Air Offensive against Germany*, (4 Vols -- Official history), London: HMSO 1961 (hereafter cited as SAO), Vol IV, p.355.

4.   Ronald W. Clark, *The Greatest Power on Earth: The Story of Nuclear Fission*, London: Sidgwick and Jackson 1980, pp.37, 137-8.

5.   CP Snow, *A Postscript to Science and Government*, London: Oxford University Press, 1962, p.29; Solly Zuckerman, *From Apes to Warlords*, 1904-1946, London: Hamish Hamilton 1978, pp.139-48.

6.   Hastings Ismay, *Memoirs*, London: Heinemann 1960, p.159.

7.   Ibid.

8.   On Churchill's close relationship with Bracken see Cecil H King, *With Malice Toward None: A War Diary*, London: Sidgwick and Jackson 1970, p.253. Declassified details of PWE are in Charles Cruickshank, *The Political Warfare Executive*, London: Davis-

Poynter, 1977. On Lockhart see RH Bruce Lockhart, *Memoirs of a British Agent*, London: Macmillan, 1974.

9. David E. Lilienthal, *The Journals of David E Lilienthal*, Vol II, "The Atomic Energy Years", 1945-1950, New York and London: Harper and Row 1964, p.10.

10. Sheila Lawlor, "Britain and the Russian entry into the war:, in Richard Langhorne (ed.) *Diplomacy and Intelligence during the Second World War*, Cambridge: Cambridge University Press 1985, p.177.

11. Elizabeth Barker, *Churchill and Eden at War*, London: Macmillan 1978, pp.22-3.

12. John Kennedy, *The Business of War*, London: Hutchinson 1957, pp.116, 178.

13. Beaverbrook to Churchill letter dated 7 February 1942, quoted in Max Hastings, *Bomber Command*, London: Michael Joseph 1980, p.114.

14. CP Snow, *Science and Government*, London: Oxford University Press 1961, p.35.

15. SAO, Vol I, p.355; SAO, Vol II, pp.110-11; Churchill to Stalin message dated 8 July 1941 reprinted in Stewart Richardson (ed.), *The Secret History of World War II: Wartime Cables and Letters of Roosevelt, Stalin, and Churchill*, New York: Richardson & Steirman / Novosti, 1986, p.3.

16. Hansard, House of Commons, 22 June 1941, 6 May 1942; SAO, Vol I, p.374; Churchill, *The Second World War*, op cit, Vol III, p.340.

17. Lawlor, op cit, pp.171, 174.

18. Martin Middlebrook, *The Berlin Raids: RAF Bomber Command -- Winter 1943-44*, London: Viking 1988, p.7; Arthur Harris, *Bomber Offensive*, London: Collins, 1947.

19. Ralph Barker, *The Thousand Plan*, London: Chatto and Windus, 1966, pp.253-4; Denis Richards & Hilary St. G Saunders, *Royal Air Force 1939-1945*, 3 Vols, London: HMSO 1954 (Official history), Vol II, pp.136-7; SAO, Vol 1, pp.405-8.

20. Longmate, op cit, p.371.

21. See Neil Orpen, *South African Forces in World War II*, (3 Vols)

Cape Town: Purnell 1971, Vol II – "War In the Desert".

22. Richards and Saunders, op cit, Vol II, pp.137-8.

23. Ralph Barker, op cit, p.262.

24. Ibid.

25. Longmate, op cit, p.369.

26. Harold Wilson, *Memoirs: The Making of a Prime Minister 1916-64*, London: Weidenfeld and Nicolson/Michael Joseph 1986, pp.122-3, 194; Irving, op cit, p.397; EG Bowen, *Radar Days*, Bristol: Adam Hilger 1987, p152.

27. Paul Kennedy, *The Rise and Fall of the Great Powers*, London: Unwin Hyman 1989, pp.357-8.

28. Hansard, House of Commons, (Army Estimates debate), 16 January 1944.

29. Henri Michel, *The Second World War*, London: Andre Deutsch 1975, p.548.

30. SAO, Vol II, pp.115-7; Richards and Saunders, op cit, Vol II, pp.286-8.

31. PRO AIR 10/3870, quoting *British Bombing Survey Unit (BBSU) Report*, p.41 paras 137-8. The *BBSU Report* was not released officially, but it is corroborated in *United States Strategic Bombing Survey (USSBS) report No.31*, "The attack on German cities", Washington DC: Government Printing Office 1945 and *USSBS Report No.64(b)* "German civilian morale". German civilian casualties are cited in: Noble & Frankland, *The Bomber Offensive Against Germany*, London: Faber 1965, p.114; Hastings, op cit, p.352 quoting German post-war Statistical Office calculations. The weight of bombs dropped and the number of homes destroyed are in SAO, Vol III, pp.117-9. The Churchill quote is from Brian Richards, *Portal of Hungerford*, London: Heinemann, 1977, p.191.

32. See Alexander Werth, *Russia at War 1941-45*, New York: Dutton, 1964.

33. See H.L Nieburg, *In the Name of Science*, Chicago: Quadrangle, 1966, pp.188-9.

Chapter 4: The Missing Front

1. David Stafford, *Military Affairs*, Vol 42, February 1978, p.29ff.
2. Vladimir Petrov (ed.), *Soviet Historians and the German Invasion*, Columbia: University of South Carolina Press 1968, p.286. The war on the eastern front has been very extensively documented by Russian historians, less so by their English-language counterparts, with only a few notable exceptions such as Werth op cit, and John Erickson, *Stalin's War With Germany*, (2 vols) London: Grafton, 1985.
3. Luftwaffe commander Adolf Galland in EM Emme (ed.), *The Impact of Air Power*, New York: Van Nostrand, 1959, pp.256-7.
4. Secret wartime correspondence disclosed in Stewart Richardson (ed.), *The Secret History of World War II: Wartime Letters and Cables of Roosevelt, Stalin, and Churchill*, New York: Richardson and Steirman / Novosti, 1986, p.6 et al.
5. Captured German documents quoted in Gordon Harrison, "The European Theatre of Operations: The Cross Channel Attack" in K.R. Greenfield (ed.) *The US Army in World War II*, (Official History) Washington: Office of the Chief of Military History, Department of the Army: US Government Printing Office 1951, p.141ff. See also Trumbull Higgins, *Winston Churchill and the Second Front*, New York: Oxford University Press, 1957, p.167-8.
6. John Winton, *Ultra at Sea*, London: Leo Cooper, 1988, pp.61-5; Dudley Saward, *Victory Denied*, London: Buchan & Enright 1985, p.219; W. Averell Harriman, *Special Envoy to Churchill and Stalin* 1941-1946, New York: Random House, 1975, p.142.
7. Alfred Price, *Aircraft versus Submarine: Anti-submarine aircraft 1912-1980*, London: Janes 1980, p.85; Terraine, op cit, pp.245, 432.
8. This account draws on CD Bekker, *Hitler's Naval War*, New York: Doubleday, 1974, based on official German records and written by a former intelligence officer in Hitler's *Kriegsmarine*. The tragedy of the Arctic convoys is curiously absent from or mentioned only cursorily in most English-language WW2 naval

history books. The Battle of the Atlantic, by contrast, has been extensively documented (see e.g. Jurgen Rohwer, "Radio Intelligence and its Role in the Battle of the Atlantic", in Christopher Andrews & David Dilks, *The Missing Dimension: Governments and Intelligence Communities in the 20th Century*, Urbana: University of Illinois Press, 1984, pp.159-168).

9. Stalin-Churchill correspondence reprinted in Richardson, op cit, pp. 6-7, 38.

10. British Air Ministry, *Origins and Development of Operation Research in the RAF*, Air Publication 3368, London: HMSO 1963, p.53.

11. RG Lee (ed.), *Guided Weapons, Battlefield Weapons Systems*, London: Brassey 1987; Ian V. Hogg and J.B. King, *German and Allied Secret Weapons of World War II*, London: Phoebus 1976, p.69.

12. See Alfred Price, *Instruments of Darkness: A History of Electronic Warfare*, London: Macdonald and Jane's 1977.

13. Hastings, op cit, pp.194, 374; Alexander McKee, *The Mosquito Log*, London: Souvenir, 1988; Richards and Saunders, op cit, Vol III, pp.152, 381-2; SAO Vol III, p.197 and Vol IV, p.428.

14. AJP Taylor, *The Second World War*, London: Hamish Hamilton, p.79; SAO, Vol IV, p.440; Terraine, op cit, pp.521-37; Harris, op cit, p.268.

15. United States Strategic Bombing Survey, Military Analysis Division, "Description of RAF Bombing", Washington DC: Government Printing Office 1945, p.1; Ministry of Defence, Air Historical Branch, *The RAF in the Bombing Offensive Against Germany*, Index No. AHB/11/117/1(b), p.122; David MacIsaac, *Strategic Bombing in World War II*, New York: Garland 1976, p.12.

16. Hansard, House of Commons, 4 March 1942, speech by Parliamentary backbencher Garro Jones MP for Aberdeen.

17. Beaverbrook quoted in George Bruce, *Second Front Now: The Road to D-Day*, London: McDonald and Janes 1979, p.27.

18. Harriman, op cit, p.137.

19. The intelligence failures are detailed in CP Stacey, *Six Years of War*, (Canadian official history) Ottawa: Government Publications 1957, p.398.

20. This account draws on: Stacey, ibid; Terence Robertson, *Dieppe, the Shame and the Glory*, London: Hutchinson 1963; Ross Munro, *Gauntlet to Overlord: The Story of the Canadian Army*, Toronto: Macmillan, 1946; John Grigg, *The Victory that Never Was*, London: Eyre Methuen 1980, p.215; Harriman, op cit, p.176ff.

21. Lawlor in Langhorne, op cit, p.173.

22. Churchill, Second World War, Vol 4, p.467.

23. Arthur Bryant, *The Turn of the Tide*, London: Collins 1957, p.487.

24. Ralph Bennett, *Ultra and Mediterranean Strategy 1941-1945*, London: Bodley Head 1981, p.162; cf., Hinsley, op cit, Vol II, p.59; Winterbotham, op cit, p.24.

25. Bennett, *Ultra and Mediterranean Strategy*, pp. 154-61; Richardson, op cit, p.86.

26. See Alan Foster, "The Times and Appeasement", *Journal of Contemporary History*, Vol 16, 1981, pp.441-65.

27. Gar Alperovitz, "How Did the Cold War Begin?" in Walter LaFeber (ed.) *The Origins of the Cold War 1941-1947*, New York: John Wiley 1971, p.18.

28. Soviet archive material released to the Western media in 1990; East German archive material quoted in Bob Edwards and Kenneth Dunne, *Study of a Master Spy*, London: Housemans 1961, p.38.

29. Arnold Toynbee, *A Study of History*, 10 Vols, Oxford: Oxford University Press 1954, Vol X, p.227

30. McLaine, op cit, p.207.

Chapter 5: The Lost Command

1. This account of the Hamburg firestorm draws on Martin Middlebrook, *The Battle of Hamburg*, London: Allen Lane 1973; Martin Middlebrook and Chris Everitt, *Bomber Command War Diaries*, London: Viking 1985, pp.410-12; Gordon Musgrove,

Operation Gomorrah: The Hamburg Firestorm Raids, London: Janes 1981; Harris, op cit, p.176; SAO, Vol II, p.236.

2.   On Los Alamos see Rhodes, op cit, p.471.

3.   SAO, Vol IV, pp.155-60.

4.   SAO, Vol II, p.28.

5.   SAO, Vol II, pp.207-8; Longmate, op cit, p.280.

6.   Martin Middlebrook, *The Nuremberg Raid*, London: Allen Lane 1973, pp.79, 96-7, 259, 274-6; James Campbell, *The Bombing of Nuremberg*, London: Futura 1974, p.159; SAO, Vol II, pp.207-8.

7.   Donald Bennett, Pathfinder, London: Muller 1958, p.210.

8.   Middlebrook, Berlin Raids, p.9.

9.   The Kassel raid is described in Hastings, op cit, 212.

10.   American losses are in Churchill, op cit, Vol V, p.461.

11.   PRO AIR 2/7852, Secretary of State for Air to Chief of Air Staff, 28 October 1943.

12.   WF Craven and JL Cate, *The Army Air Forces in World War II*, (7 vols), Chicago: University of Chicago, 1948-1958, Vol III, p.320.

13.   Hansard, House of Commons, 1 December 1943.

14.   SAO, Vol III, p.82.

15.   Hastings, op cit, pp.302-6, 324-5.

16.   SAO, Vol 4, pp.144, 148.

17.   Quoted in R Beaumont, "The Bomber Offensive as a Second Front", *Journal of Contemporary History*, 22 January 1987, p.6.

18.   PRO AIR 20/8152, Portal memorandum dated 1 August 1944 and Chiefs of Staff (COS) meeting 261(0) of 5 August 1944.

19.   Albert Speer, *Inside the Third Reich*, London: Weidenfeld, 1970, p.286.

20.   Henri Michel, *The Second World War*, London: Andre Deutsch, 1975, p.549.

21.   Denis Richards, *Portal of Hungerford*, London: Heinemann, 1978, pp.318-24.

22.   Craven & Cate, op cit, Vol 6, pp.352, 423; SAO, Vol 4, pp.501-3; MM Postan, *British War Production* (Official history), London: HMSO, 1958, pp.484-5

23.   LF Ellis, *Victory in the West*, (official history 6 vols), London:

HMSO, 1968, Vol I, p.430.

24.   Zuckerman, op cit, p.340.

25.   Michel, op cit, p.549.

26.   Georgi Zhukov, *Reminiscences and Reflections*, (2 vols), Moscow: Progress 1985, Vol II, pp.338, 345-7; cf., Arthur William Tedder, *With Prejudice*, London: Cassell 1966, p.506.

27.   McLaine, op cit, p.244.

28.   Henry Pelling, *The British Communist Party: A Historical Profile*, London: Adam and Charles Black, 1975, pp. 120-1.

29.   McLaine, op cit, pp.206-7.

30.   Quoted in M Smith, *British Air Strategy Between the Wars*, Oxford: Clarendon, 1984, p.64.

Part Two: Cold War 1944-1990

Chapter 6: War in the Shadows

1.   The figures are from: Churchill, op cit, Vol IV, p.832; John Kennedy, op cit, p.325; Paul Kennedy, op cit, pp.352, 354; Liddell Hart, op cit, p.559; Zhukov, Vol II, pp.307, 344; US Army newspaper *Stars and Stripes*, 15 May 1945. Also of interest is Günter Bischof, *Die Invasion in der Normandie 1944*, Innsbruck: Studienverlag, 2002.

2.   John Kennedy, ibid.,

3.   David Fraser, *And We Shall Shock Them: The British Army in the Second World War*, London: Hodder and Stoughton 1983, p.348.

4.   The account of the Arnhem operation draws on: Cornelius Ryan, *A Bridge Too Far*, London: Hamish Hamilton, 1974; Ralph Bennett, "Ultra and Some Command Decisions", *Journal of Contemporary History*, Vol 16, 1981, pp.145-6; Richard Lamb, *Montgomery in Europe 1943-45*, London: Buchan and Enright 1983, p.227.

5.   PRO AIR 37/876, Arthur Coningham, "Operations Carried out by the Second Tactical Air Force between 6th June 1944

and 9 May 1945", p.23.

6.   Ryan, op cit, p.454.

7.   Bennett, op.cit, "Ultra and Some Command Decisions", p.135; Liddell Hart, op cit, p.536.

8.   The account of the Italian campaign draws on: Martin Blumenson, *Anzio*: Philadelphia: Lippencott, 1963: Peter Calvocoressi and Guy Wint, *Total War: Causes and Courses of the Second World War*, Harmondsworth: Penguin 1986, pp. 511-2; Bennett, *Ultra and Mediterranean Strategy*, p.264; Fraser, op cit, p.282.

9.   Albrecht Kesselring, *Memoirs*, London: Greenhill 1988, p.193.

10.   Leslie Groves, *Now It Can Be Told*, New York: Harper and Row 1962, p.184.

11.   Elizabeth Barker, op cit, p.236.

12.   Letter from Smuts to Churchill dated 31 August 1943, quoted in Churchill, *The Second World War*, Vol V, p.112.

13.   Chiefs of Staff quoted in Michael Balfour, *The Adversaries: America, Russia and the Open World 1941-1962*, London: Routledge, Kegan Paul 1981, p.9.

14.   SAO, Vol III, p.252.

15.   SAO, Vol III, p.108; David Irving, *The Destruction of Dresden*, London: Kimber 1963, pp.88, 106-7, 256.

16.   Hastings, op cit, pp.340-4; Irving, *Destruction of Dresden*, pp.173-7, 206, 225-32, 236; Middlebrook and Everitt, op cit, pp.663-4.

17.   Richards and Saunders, Vol III, p.270; Irving, *Destruction of Dresden*, pp.173, 206; SAO, Vol III, p.109.

18.   Janusz Piekalkiewicz, *The Air War 1939-1945*, Poole: Blandford 1985, p.402.

19.   See *United States Strategic Bombing Survey*, "Area Studies Division Report No.1", Washington: Government Printers 1945, pp.235-40, Alan S. Milward, *War, Economy and Society*, London: Allen Lane 1982, p.302.

20.   Hastings, op. cit.p.342.

21.   Churchill memorandum to Air Minister Sinclair, 26 January 1945 quoted in SAO, Vol III, p.103; Deputy Air Minister Sir

Norman Bottomley to Harris, 27 January 1945 quoted in SAO, Vol III, p.103.

22. Longmate, op cit, p.335.
23. SAO, Vol III, pp.105-6.
24. Hastings, op cit, p.342; Irving, *Destruction of Dresden*, pp. 148, 158, 206; Piekalkiewicz, op cit, p.402.
25. See PRO AIR 37/876, Air Chief Marshal Sir Trafford Leigh-Mallory, "Operations Carried Out by Second Tactical Air Force, 6 June 1944 to 9 May 1945".
26. Longmate, op cit, p.342.
27. SAO, Vol III, pp.113-4.
28. Hansard, House of Commons, 6 March 1945.
29. Ibid.
30. Richards and Saunders, op cit, Vol III, p.268.
31. Hastings, op cit, p.337; Piekalkiewics, op cit, pp.403-5.
32. See Hinsley, op cit, Vol II, Appendix 5, pp.671-2.
33. SAO, Vol III, pp.113-4.
34. Randolph S. Churchill and Martin Gilbert, *Winston S Churchill*, (8 vols), London: Heinemann, 1954-1988, Vol VIII, p.259.
35. The capture of Berlin is described in Zhukov, op cit, Vol II, p.347 et al.
36. See generally Alexander Werth, *Russia at War 1941-1945*, New York: Avon 1965; John Erickson, *Stalin's War With Germany*, (2 vols) London: Grafton, 1985 where individual campaigns are listed at Vol II, p.1181. Total losses of the German Wehrmacht were 72 percent of its officers and men. Most died on the Soviet-German front.

Chapter 7: Atomic Blackmail

1. Liddell Hart, op cit, p.691; Piekalkiewicz, op cit, 404-6, 424.
2. Lillian Wald Kay, "Public Opinion and the Bomb", *Journal of Educational Sociology*, No 22, January 1949, pp.357-60.
3. *New York Times*, 30 August 1945.

4.   *New York Times*, 24 July 1941.
5.   DF Fleming, *The Cold War and Its Origins: 1917-1960*, New York: Random 1961, p.270.
6.   See generally Balfour, op cit., For Russian losses see Erickson, op cit, individual campaigns listed at Vol II, p.1181.
7.   The account of Gehlen's US visit is based on: Christopher Simpson, *Blowback: America's Recruitment of Nazis and Its Effects on the Cold War*, London: Weidenfeld and Nicolson 1988, pp.42, 44; Danil Kraminov, *The Spring of 1945: Notes of a Soviet War Correspondent*, Moscow: Novosti 1985, pp.99-102; Richard Harris Smith, *OSS*, Berkeley: University of California Press 1972, p.240. For a fuller account of Gehlen see EH Cookridge, *Gehlen: Spy of the Century*, London: Hodder and Stoughton, 1971, which relies on Soviet and East German archive material. Also of interest is: All-Party Parliamentary War Crimes Group, *Report on the Entry of Nazi War Criminals and Collaborators into the United Kingdom 1945-1950*, London: HMSO, 1988.
8.   Marlis G Steinert, "The Allied Decision to Arrest the Donitz Goverment", *Historical Journal*, Vol 31 No 3, 1988, p. 658-60.
9.   Steinert, op cit, p.272.
10.   David Fraser, *Alanbrooke*, London: Collins, 1982, p.489.
11.   Steinert, op cit, p.272.
12.   Gar Alperovitz, "Atomic Diplomacy, *The Listener*, 10 August 1989, p.6.
13.   Barton Bernstein, (ed.), *Politics and Policies of the Truman Administration*, Chicago: University of Chicago Press 1970; *New York Times*, 9 August 1945.
14.   Churchill, *Second World* War, Vol VI, p.553.
15   Y Larionov, N Yeronin, B Solovyov, V. Timokhovich, *World War II Decisive Battles of the Soviet Army*, Moscow: Progress 1984, p.452.
16.   Bernstein, op cit, p.32.
17.   Churchill, *Second World War*, Vol VI, p.553.
18.   Byrnes to US Navy Secretary James Forrestal, diary entry 28 July 1945 in Walter Millis (ed.) *The Forrestal Diaries*, New York:

Viking 1951.

19. See Robert J. Butow, *Japan's Decision to Surrender*, Stanford: Stanford University Press 1954, p.112; Liddel Hart, op cit, p.693.

20. *New York Times*, 6 September 1945; see Wilfred Burchett, *Shadows of Hiroshima*, London: Verso 1983, p.69 quoting Japanese figures; and cf., generally United States Strategic Bombing Survey, "The Effects of Atomic Bombs on Hiroshima and Nagasaki", Washington DC: Government Printing Office 1946.

21. Burchett, op cit, pp.44-5.

22. *United States Strategic Bombing Survey*, "The Effects of Atomic Bombs on Hiroshima and Nagasaki", p.483.

23. Dwight D Eisenhower, *The White House Years*, London: Heinemann, 1963, p.483.

24. Churchill, *Second World War*, Vol VI, p.559.

25. US State Department, "Conference on Potsdam", *Foreign Relations of the United States 1945*, Washington DC: Government Printing Office 1969, p.485; Butow, op cit, p. 112; Liddel Hart, op cit, p.693.

26. Douglas Botting, *From the Ruins of the Reich: Germany 1945-1949* (New York: New American Library, 1985, p,138

Chapter 8: Banishing the *'Banditti'*

1. Churchill, *Second World War*, Vol V, pp.539-44.

2. Prokopis Papastratis, "The British and the Greek Resistance Movements EAM and EDES", in Marion Sarafis (ed.), *Greece: From Resistance to Civil War*, Nottingham: Spokesman 1980, p.36.

3. Christopher M Woodhouse, *The Struggle for Greece 1941-1949*, London: Hart-Davis 1976, pp.3-34, 76-7; LS Stavrianos, "The Greek National Liberation Front (EAM): A Study in Resistance, Organisation and Administration", *Journal of Modern History*, March 1952, pp.42-55.

4. See Lawrence S Wittner, *American Intervention in Greece 1943-1949*,

New York: Columbia, 1982; John O Iatrides (ed), *Greece in the 1940s: A Nation in Crisis*, Hanover and London: University Press of New England, 1981; Howard Jones, *A New Kind of War: America's global strategy and the Truman Doctrine in Greece*, London: Oxford University Press 1989.

5.   *The Times*, 17 November 1971, quoting US Senator Lee Metcalf who denounced American aid to "a military regime of collaborators and Nazi sympathisers".

6.   William M Leary (ed,) *The Central Intelligence Agency: History and Documents*, Alabama: University of Alabama Press, 1984, pp.131-33.

7.   Yiannis Roubatis and Karen Wynn, "CIA Operations in Greece", in Philip Agee and Louis Wolf (eds), *Dirty Work: The CIA in Western Europe*, London: Zed, 1981, pp.147-157.

8.   Quoted in Bruce R Kuniholm, *Origins of the Cold War in the Near East*, Princeton: Princeton University Press 1980, p.411.

9.   Ibid.

10.   Information provided by Simon Wiesenthal Centre, Los Angeles, in written correspondence with the author, 1990.

11.   Simpson, op cit, p.91.

12.   Simpson, op cit, pp.89-90.

13.   See HC Butcher, *My Three Years with Eisenhower*, New York: Doubleday 1946, p.422; NS Jucker, "Italy: East or West", *Political Quarterly*, Vol XXII April-June 1951, pp.175-85.

14.   See Roland Flamini, *Pope, Premier, President*, New York: Macmillan, 1980.

15.   See Alexander Ramati, *The Assisi Underground*, London: Sphere 1981.

16.   See John Cornwell, *Hitler's Pope: The secret history of Pius XII*, Harmondsworth: Penguin, 1999.

17.   Simon Wiesenthal, *SS Colonel Walter Rauff: The Church Connection 1943-1947*, Los Angeles: Simon Wiesenthal Center, May 1984; *Boston Globe*, 28 May 1984 quoting US intelligence documents accessed under the American Freedom of Information Act; *Latin America Weekly Report*, 11 February 1983. On Barbie and

Eichmann see: *William Stevenson, The Bormann Brotherhood*, New York: Harcourt, Brace 1973, pp.181,198; Ian Sayer and Douglas Botting, *America's Secret Army: The Story of Counter-intelligence Corps*, London: Grafton 1989, pp.373-82.

18. William Blum, *The CIA: A Forgotten History*, London: Zed 1986, p.26.

19. John Cooney, *The American Pope: The Life and Times of Francis Cardinal Spellman*, New York: Times Books, 1984, p.160.

20. See; Association of Asian Studies, "Anti-Japanese Movements in Southeast Asia during World War II". Abstract (1996) www.aasianst.org/absts/1996abst/inter/i181.htm [Accessed 21 July 2003]

21. See Yoji Akashi, "MPAJA/Force 136 Resistance Against the Japanese in Malaya, 1941-1945". Association of Asian Studies. Abstract (1996) www.aasianst.org/absts/1996abst/inter/intertoc.htm [Accessed 21 July 2003].

22. *Kodansha Encyclopedia of Japan*, (9 vols) Tokyo and New York: Dondasha 1983, Vol VII, p.202.

23. Harry S Truman, *Memoirs*, (2 vols), New York: Doubleday 1956, Vol II, p.66.

24. See LF Stone, *The Hidden History of the Korean War*, New York: Monthly Review Press, 1952.

25. See generally John Halliday and Bruce Cummings, *Korea: The Unknown War*, London: Viking 1988.

26. Max Hastings, *The Korean War*, London: Michael Joseph, 1987, p.xiii.

27. Dean Acheson, *Present at the Creation*, New York: W.W. Norton 1969, p.374. NSC-68 was declassified in 1977.

28. US Department of State, *Foreign Relations of the United States*, 1950, Vol I, "Korea", pp.73-4, 920-21.

29. *Bulletin of the American Society of Newspaper Editors*, Winter 1951.

30. See Wilfred Burchett, *Passport: An Autobiography*, Melbourne: Nelson 1969, Chapter 19 "Germ Warfare".

31. John W. Powell, "Japan's Biological Weapons: 1930-1945", *Bulletin of Atomic Scientists*, October 1980; and see generally Peter

Williams and David Wallace, *Unit 731: The Japanese Army's Secret*, London: Hodder and Stoughton 1989.

32. Quoted in Blum, op cit, p.22.

33. Alfred McCoy, *The Politics of Heroin in Southeast Asia*, New York: Harper, 1972, pp.92-109, 306-8; cf., *New York Times Book Review*, 3 September 1972, for an account of official attempts to suppress publication of McCoy's book, considered by the CIA to be "damaging to the interests" of the US.

34. Christopher Robbins, *Air America: The Story of the CIA's Secret Airlines*, New York: Putnam's 1979, p.237, 239-40, n.13.

35. Marchetti and Marks, op cit, pp.158-60.

36. Trevor Barnes, "The Secret Cold War: CIA and American Foreign Policy 1946-56, *Historical Journal*, Vol 25, No.3, September 1982; John Prados, *Presidents' Secret Wars: CIA and Pentagon Covert Operations Since World War II*, New York: William Morrow, 1986; Myron J. Smith (ed.), *The Secret Wars*, (3 vols), Santa Barbara: ABC-Clio, 1981, Vol II, pp.xvi-xviii.

37. See Stephen Schlesinger and Stephen Kinzer, *Bitter Fruit: The American Coup in Guatemala*, London: Sinclair Browne, 1982.

38. Frank Kitson, *Low Intensity Operations: Subversion, Insurgency and Peacekeeping*, London: Faber, 1971, p.87. On Vietnam see Larry Cable, *Conflict of Myths: The Development of American Counter-Insurgency Doctrine and the Vietnam War*, New York: New York University Press 1986, p.82.

39. Copies of documents in the possession of the author, seized from OAS fugitives by leftist officers of the Armed Forces Movement (AFM) in Lisbon following their 1973 coup that overthrew the right-wing Salazar regime and led to the formation of a socialist government in Portugal. Further information obtained in a series of interviews conducted by the author with senior AFM officers in Lisbon. Also of interest is: D Kendo, "Comores: L'Ordre Mercenaire", *Jeune Afrique*, no. 1511/1512, December 1989; cf., Economist Intelligence Unit (EIU), *Madagascar, Comoros, Country Profile, 1989-90*, London 1990, pp 32-36; EIU, *Madagascar, Mauritius,*

Seychelles, Comoros: Country Report No. 1, London 1990.
40. Documents in possession of the author.

Chapter 9: Weapons of Mass Distraction

1. George M Kahin, *Intervention: How America Became Involved in Vietnam*, New York: Knopf, 1986, p.205; Herman and Chomsky, op cit, pp.206-10.

2. *Washington Post*, "US Faked '65 Evidence on War in Vietnam" quoting ex-CIA officer, 20 March 1982.

3. On Vietnam generally see Bernard Fall, *Street Without Joy*, London: Michael Joseph, 1972; Neil Sheehan, *A Bright Shining Lie*, London: Jonathan Cape 1989.

4. A detailed account of Operation Phoenix is provided by ex-CIA officer Frank Snepp, *Decent Interval*, New York: Vintage Books, 1978; cf., John Pilger, *A Secret Country*, London: Jonathan Cape 1989, p.133.

5. Suppressed CIA report quoted in House of Representatives select investigative committee (chairman Otis Pike) report "The Pike Papers". See Final Report of the Select Committee to Study Governmental Operations with respect to Intelligence Activities, 26 April 1976, Vol 1, "Foreign and Military Intelligence" Washington: US Government Printing Office, 1976. See also "The CIA Report the President Doesn't Want You to Read", *Village Voice*, 23 February 1976, p.445; and cf., *Village Voice* 16 February 1976 and 26 February 1976.

6. Myron J Smith, op cit, Vol II, pp.xvi-xviii.

7. See generally Prados, op cit.

8. Stewart Steven, *Operation Splinter Factor*, London: Hodder and Stoughton 1974, pp.98-99, 131. On the origins of RFE/RL see: Robert T Holt, *Radio Free Europe*, Minneapolis: University of Minneapolis 1958, p.12; cf., David Wise and Thomas Ross, *The Invisible Government*, New York: Vintage 1964, p.326ff; Marchetti and Marks, op cit, pp.174-78. RFE/RL budget is in *New York*

Times, 15 March 1971.

9.   Steven, op cit, pp.100-1.

10. Simpson, op cit, p.126.

11. See Allan Ryan, *Quiet Neighbours,* New York: Harcourt Brace 1984, pp.26-7.

12. See Simpson, op cit, pp. 89, 108, 124, 125-36,177, 184, 201, 205, 219, 224, 247-8, 267, 269 -- citing classified information made available to Simpson under the US Freedom of Information Act.

13. Lyn Smith, "Covert British Propaganda: The Information Research Department, 1947-1977", *Millennium,* Vol IX 1980, p.72 et al.

14. Ibid.

15. Ibid.

16. Ray Merrick, "The Russian Committee of the British Foreign Office and the Cold War, 1946-1947", *Journal of Contemporary History,* Vol 20, 1985, pp.453-468, quoting PRO Foreign Office files FO 371/71687 & PRO FO 371/77623.

17. Anthony Cavendish, *Inside Intelligence,* London: Palu 1987, p.55. This book written by a former senior British intelligence agent was initially banned by the British government. The ban was lifted in 1989. On British operations aimed at the Baltic States see generally Tom Bower, *The Red Web,* London: Aurum 1989; Kim Philby, *My Silent War,* London: Macgibbon and Kee, 1968.

18. See Wesley K Wark, "Coming in from the Cold: British Propaganda and Red Army Defectors, 1945-1952, *International History Review,* Vol IX No. 1, February 1987, pp.54-71, and cf., Appendix II listing numbers and reasons for defection; Anthony Verrier, *Through the Looking Glass: British Foreign Policy in the Age of Illusions,* London: Jonathan Cape 1983, p.52.

19. Steven, op cit, pp. 98-101, 131.

20. Thomas C Sorensen, *The Word War: The story of American propaganda,* New York, Harper and Row, 1968, pp.69-70.

21. Simpson, op cit, pp.224-5ff.

22. Confirmed by former senior CIA executive in *Saturday Evening*

Post, 22 May 1967, p.12.

23. Presidential Study: Commission on International Broadcasting, 1973, Congressional Record -- Extensions of Remarks, November 17, 1981, p.E5361.

24. Classified 1976 US congressional committee report "Covert Relationships with the United States Media", leaked to the media and published in full by *Rolling Stone*, 20 October 1979, pp.65, 68.

25. Ibid, *Rolling Stone*, p.67.

26. This account summarises the marathon US congressional inquiry into the Iran-Contra affair which ended in 1989 and resulted in 8 500 pages of transcript.

27. Goodman in testimony at official investigation into CIA-media activities, "The Gates Hearings", Washington, Sept-Oct 1991.

28. WACL conference document in possession of the author.

29. Ibid.

30. "Reagan cites KAL jet in arguing for buildup", *International Herald Tribune*, 22 September 1983.

31. "Outrage over jet propels arms bill", *Guardian*, 3 November 1983.

32. The Iran-Contra affair is well documented in Jonathan Marshall, Peter Dale Scott, Jane Hunter, *The Iran-Contra Connection: Secret teams and covert operations in the Reagan era*, Boston: South End Press, 1987. For further discussion see Gregory F Treverton, *Covert Action: The CIA and the limits of American intervention in the post-war world*, London: IB Taurus, 1987

Part Three: New World Disorder 1991-2004

Chapter 10: 'Humanitarian' Crusades

1. See Gordon Wright, *The Ordeal of Total War*, New York: Harper and Row, 1968, pp.264-5.

2. See generally Charles Higham, *Trading with the Enemy*, London:

Robert Hale, 1983.

3.   "Soviet Military Spending: Assessing the Numbers Game", *International Security*, Vol 6, No.4 Spring 1982, pp. 78-101; *New York Times*, 7 March 1985; *Business Week*, "Pentagon spending is the economy's biggest gun", 2 October 1985, p.60; Solly Zuckerman, "Technology for a Cold War" in Richard Crockatt and Steve Smith (eds.), *The Cold War Past and Present*, London: Allen and Unwin 1987, p.30; Hugh Thomas, *Armed Truce: The Beginnings of the Cold War 1945-46*, London: Hamish Hamilton 1986, p.441.

4.   Estimate quoted in Treverton, op cit, p.14.

5.   *Los Angeles Times*, 8 April 1990.

6.   *Guardian*, 22 July 1989; *Observer*, 16 April 1989, 17 December 1989; *New Statesman*, 10 April 1987, p.14; Lawrence Freedman, *US Intelligence and the Soviet Strategic Threat*, London: Macmillan 1977, p.197.

7.   *Guardian*, "US refrained from warning off Saddam", 12 September 1990; Milton Viorst, "Report from Baghdad", *New Yorker*, 24 September 1990, p.90; John Pilger "Sins of Omission", *New Statesman*, 8 January 1991, p.8.

8.   *Financial Times*, 11 February 1991, p.2; *Newsweek*, 8 April 1991, pp.14-8.

9.   Ray Takeyh and Nikolas Gvosdev, "Do terrorist networks need a home?", *Washington Quarterly*, Summer 2002. Also of interest are Gerald Knaus and Felix Martin, "Lessons from Bosnia and Herzegovina: Travails of the European Raj", *Journal of Democracy*, July 2003, Volume 14, Number 3; Kofi Annan, "International action to uphold human rights requires a new understanding of state and individual sovereignty", *Financial Times*, 31 December 1999; Peter Ford, "Few borders sacred to new UN", *Christian Science Monitor*, 29 September 1999.

10.   Cees Wiebes, *Intelligence and the War in Bosnia 1992-1995*, Amsterdam: Lit Verlag, 2003. First published by Netherlands Institute of War Documentation (NIOD) in April 2002.

Summarised in Richard J Aldrich, "America used Islamists to arm the Bosnian Muslims", *Guardian*, 22 April 2002.

11. See generally David Chandler, *From Kosovo to Kabul: Human Rights and International Intervention*, London: Pluto Press, 2002.

12. *New York Times Magazine*, April 6, 1980, pp. 28, 29.

13. See *Undeclared War: Armed Intervention and other Forms of Interference in the Internal Affairs of the Democratic Republic of Afghanistan*, Kabul: Government Information Office, 1984.

14. Oil statistics taken from: Viktor Samarin, *Regional Conflicts*, Moscow: Novosti, 1987, p.14; *United States National Energy Policy: Report of the National Energy Policy Development Group*, May 2001, www.whitehouse.gov [Accessed January 2002].

15. See generally *Undeclared War*, op cit.

Chapter 11: The Haunting of America

1. See Adam Dolnik and Kimberly McCloud, "Debunk the myth of al-Qaeda", *Christian Science Monitor*, 23 May 2002; Jason Burke, "What is al-Qaeda?", *Observer*, 13 July 2003.

2. See Seymour M Hersh, "The Other War", *New Yorker*, 12 April, 2004.

3. See Barnett Rubin, "Rebuilding Afghanistan: The folly of stateless democracy", *Current History*, April 2004.

4. "Government Accounts of 9/11 Reveal Gaps, Inconsistencies", *Wall Street Journal*, 29 March 2004; cf., *Washington Post*, March 22, 2004.

5. *National Security Strategy of the United States*, Washington: US State Department, September 2002, p.28.

6. *Independent*, (London) April 2, 2004.

7. Richard Clarke, *Against All Enemies*, New York: Simon and Schuster, 2004, p.63.

8. Robert Baer, *Sleeping With the Devil*, New York: Crown, 2003.

9. Jason Burke, *Al-Qaeda: Casting a Shadow of Terror*, London: IB Tauris, 2003, pp.93, 98, 103, 199. Also of interest is James

Buchan, "Inside the mind of a terrorist", *Observer*, 16 September, 2001.

10.   Craig Pyes, Josh Meyer and William C Rempel, "Terrorists use Bosnia as base and sanctuary", *Los Angeles Times*, 7 October 2001.

11.   Ibid.,

12.   Ibid.,

Chapter 12: Profits of Doom

1.   AFP newswire, 7 May 2003.

2.   John Kampfner, "Saving Private Lynch story flawed", BBC, London, 18 May 2003.

3.   *Los Angeles Times*, 20 May 2003.

4.   *Guardian*, Oct. 9, 2002.

5.   *New York Times*, June 5, 2003; *Washington Post* , June 7, 2003.

6.   Knight Ridder Newspapers, Washington Bureau, March 15, 2004.

7.   Knight Ridder Newspapers, Washington Bureau, March 15, 2004 quoting a copy of a letter it had obtained, dated June 26, 2002, from the INC to the US Senate Appropriations Committee which funded the INC. A list of 108 articles that the Iraqi National Congress itself admitted were based on information it supplied to news media is available on the web at www.krwashington.com

8.   Knight Ridder Newspapers, Washington Bureau, March 15, 2004.

9.   *Washington Post*, 26 May 2003.

10.   *Guardian*, October 19, 2001.

11.   UN weapons inspector Scott Ritter, "A Weapons Cache We'll Never See", *New York Times*, 25 August 2003.

12.   *New Yorker*, 6 May 2003.

13.   *LA Weekly*, 20 - 26 February, 2004.

14.   Ibid.,

15. *Time*, 9 June 2003

16. See *Le Figaro*, 15 February 2003; *Le Monde*, 10 and 20 March 2003; *Le Monde diplomatique*, English language edition, March 2003.

17. "UK to Aid DU Removal," BBC News, April 23, 2003; "Allied Troops 'Risk Uranium Exposure," *Financial Times*, April 25, 2003; "Uranium Warheads May Leave Both Sides a Legacy of Death for Decades," *Los Angeles Times*, 30 March, 2003; "U.S. Forces' Use of Depleted Uranium Is Illegal," *Glasgow Sunday Herald*, 30 March, 2003.

18. Dr Doug Rokke, "Gulf War Casualties", on line at www.rense.com/general29/gulf.htm [Accessed September 30, 2002].

19. UN weapons inspector Scott Ritter, "A Weapons Cache We'll Never See", *New York Times*, 25 August 2003.

20. *Guardian*, October 17, 2003.

21. "The Corporate Military", *Business Week* (US), 15 September 2003.

22. For further discussion see Richard Duncan, *The Dollar Crisis: Causes, Consequences, Cures,* London: New York: John Wiley & Sons, 2003; Michel Chossudovsky, "Euro versus Dollar: Rivalry Between America and "Old Europe", *Global Outlook*, No 5, Fall 2003; William F Engdahl, "A New American Century? Iraq and the hidden euro-dollar wars," *Current Concerns*, No 4, June 2003.

23. Figures from *Economist*, July 5, 2003.

Chapter 13: The Future: Right Here, Right Now

1. Donald Kagan, Gary Schmitt, Thomas Donnelly (eds.), *Rebuilding America's Defenses: Strategies, Forces and Resources For A New Century*, Washington: Project for the New American Century (PNAC). September 2000, p.14.

2. Kagan, Schmitt, Donnelly, op cit, p. 64.
3. Kagan, Schmitt, Donnelly, op cit, p. 55.
4. Kagan, Schmitt, Donnelly, op cit, p.51.
5. The full text of the US national security strategy is available online at www.whitehouse.gov/nsc/nss.htm.
6. Noam Chomsky, "Dominance and its Dilemmas", *Le Monde Diplomatique*, August 2003.
7. Ibid.,
8. See Peter Mair and Ingrid van Biezen, "Party Membership in Twenty European Democracies 1980-2000", *Party Politics*, Vol 7, No 1, 2001, pp.5-21.

Selected Bibliography

Alperowitz, Gar, *Atomic Diplomacy:* Hiroshima and Potsdam, London: Secker and Warburg, 1965

Barber, Noel, *Sinister Twilight:* The Fall of Singapore, London: Collins, 1969

Barker, Elizabeth, *Churchill and Eden at War,* London: Macmillan, 1978

Barker, Ralph, *The Thousand Plan,* London: Chatto and Windus, 1966

Bennett, Ralph, *Ultra in the West,* London: Hutchinson, 1979

Bennett, Ralph, *Ultra and Mediterranean Strategy 1941-1945,* London: Hamish Hamilton, 1989

Bernstein, Barton (ed.), *Politics and Policies of the Truman Administration,* Chicago: University of Chicago Press, 1970

Blum, William, *The CIA: A Forgotten History,* London: Zed, 1986

Burchett, Wilfred, *Shadows of Hiroshima,* London: Verso 1983

Butow, Robert J, *Japan's Decision to Surrender,* Stanford: Stanford University Press 1954, p.112

Churchill, Winston S, *The Second World War,* (6 vols) London: Cassell, 1948-1954

Clark, Ronald W, *The Greatest Power on Earth,* London: Sidgwick and Jackson, 1980

Craven, WF and Cate JL, *The Army Air Forces in World War 11,* (7 vols), Chicago: University of Chicago, 1948-1958

Erickson, John, *Stalin's War With Germany*, (2 vols), London: Grafton, 1985

Fraser, David, *Alanbrooke*, London: Collins, 1982

Fraser, David, *And We Shall Shock Them: The British Army in the Second World War*, London: Hodder and Stoughton, 1983

Groves, Leslie, *Now It Can Be Told*, New York: Harper and Row, 1962

Harriman, W Averell, *Special Envoy to Churchill and Stalin 1941-1946*, New York: Random House, 1975

Harris, Arthur, *Bomber Offensive*, London: Collins, 1947

Hart, Basil Liddell, *History of the Second World War*, London: Cassell 1965

Hastings, Max, *Bomber Command*, London: Michael Joseph, 1980

Herman, Edward S, and Chomsky, Noam, *Manufacturing Consent: The political economy of the mass media*, New York: Pantheon, 1988

Hinsley, FH, *British Intelligence in the Second World War: Its Influence on Strategy and Operations*, (Official History, 4 vols), London: HMSO 1977-1988.

Hogg, Ian V, and King JB, *German and Allied Secret Weapons of World War II*, London: Phoebus, 1976

Irving, David, *Churchill's War*, Vol 1, "The Struggle for Power", Bullsbrook (Australia): Veritas, 1987

Irving, David, *The Destruction of Dresden*, London: William Kimber, 1963

Kagan D, Schmitt G, Donnelly T (eds.), *Rebuilding America's Defenses: Strategies, Forces and Resources For A New Century*, Washington: Project for the New American Century (PNAC). September 2000

Selected Bibliography

Kennedy, John, *The Business of War*, London: Hutchinson, 1957

Kennedy, Paul, *The Rise and Fall of the Great Powers: Economic Change and Military Conflict from 1500 to 2000*, London: Unwin Hyman, 1989

Kirby, S Woodburn, *Singapore: The Chain of Disaster*, London: Cassell, 1971

Longmate, Norman, *The Bombers: The RAF Offensive Against Germany 1939-1945*, London: Hutchinson, 1983

Marchetti, Victor, and Marks, John D, *The CIA and the Cult of Intelligence*, London: Jonathan Cape, 1974

McClaine, Ian, *Ministry of Morale: Home Front Morale and the Ministry of Information in World War II*, London: Allen and Unwin, 1979

McCoy, Alfred, *The Politics of Heroin in Southeast Asia*, New York: Harper, 1972

Michel, Henri, *The Second World War*, London: Andre Deutch, 1975

Middlebrook, Martin, *The Berlin Raids: RAF Bomber Command Winter 1943-1944*, London: Viking, 1988

Middlebrook, Martin, and Everitt, Chris, *Bomber Command War Diaries: An Operational Reference Book 1939-1945*, London: Viking, 1985

Montgomery, Brian, *Shenton of Singapore*, London: Leo Cooper/Secker and Warburg, 1984

Prados, John, *Presidents' Secret Wars: CIA and Pentagon Covert Operations Since World War II*, New York: William Morrow, 1986

Piekalkiewicz, Janusz, *The Air War 1939-1945*, Poole: Blandford, 1985

Price, Alfred, *Instruments of Darkness: History of Electronic Warfare*, London Macdonald and Jane's, 1977

Rhodes, Richard, *The Making of the Atomic Bomb*, Harmondsworth: Penguin, 1988

Richards, Denis, *Portal of Hungerford*, London: Heinemann, 1978

Richards, Denis and Hilary St G Saunders, *Royal Air Force 1939-1945*, (3 vols -- Official History), London: HMSO, 1954

Richardson, Stewart (ed.), *The Secret History of World War II: Wartime Letters and Cables of Roosevelt, Stalin and Churchill*, New York: Richardson and Steirman / Novosti, 1986

Rusbridger, James, & Nave, Eric, *Betrayal at Pearl Harbor*, London: Michael O'Mara / New York: Simon & Schuster, 1991

SAO, see Webster, Charles, and Frankland, Nobel

Simpson, Christopher, *Blowback: America's Recruitment of Nazis and Its Effects on the Cold War*, London: Weidenfeld and Nicolson, 1988

Smith, Myron J (ed.), *The Secret Wars*, (3 vols), Santa Barbara: ABC-Clio, 1981

Steven, Stewart, *Operation Splinter Factor*, London: Hodder and Stoughton, 1974

Stinnert, Robert, *Day of Deceit*, New York: Free Press, 1999

Terraine, John, *A Time for Courage: The Royal Air Force in The European War 1939-1945*, New York: Macmillan, 1985

Thorne, Christopher, *Allies of a Kind: The United States, Britain and the war against Japan, 1941-1945*, London: Hamish Hamilton, 1978

Treverton, Gregory F *Covert Action: The CIA and the limits of American intervention in the post-war world*, London: I.B. Tauris, 1987

Undeclared War: Armed Intervention and other Forms of Interference in the Internal Affairs of the Democratic Republic of Afghanistan, Kabul:

Government Information Office, 1984.

United States Strategic Bombing Survey, Washington DC: Government Printing Office, 1945

Webster, Charles, and Frankland, Noble, *The Strategic Air Offensive against Germany*, (4 vols) London: HMSO, 1961.

Wilson, Harold *Memoirs: The Making of a Prime Minister 1916-1964*, London: Weidenfeld and Nicolson/Michael Joseph, 1986

Winterbotham, Frederick W, *The Ultra Secret*, London: Weidenfeld and Nicolson, 1974

Zhukov, Georgi, *Reminiscences and Reflections*, (2 Vols), Moscow: Progress, 1985

Zuckerman, Solly, *From Apes to Warlords*, 1904-1946, London: Hamish Hamilton, 1978

SELECTED JOURNAL ARTICLES

Bennett, Ralph, "Ultra and Some Command Decisions", *Journal of Contemporary History*, Vol 16, 1981

Smith, Lyn, "Covert British Propaganda: The Information Research Department, 1947-1977", *Millennium*, Vol IX 1980

Steinert, Marlis G, "The Allied Decision to Arrest the Donitz Goverment", *Historical Journal*, Vol 31 No 3, 1988

Wark, Wesley K, "Coming in from the Cold: British Propaganda and Red Army Defectors, 1945-1952, *International History Review*, Vol IX No. 1, February 1987

Index:

Index